T0312271

Cambridge Elements ≡

Elements in Applied Evolutionary Science
edited by
David F. Bjorklund
Florida Atlantic University

ATTACHMENT AND PARENT-OFFSPRING CONFLICT

Origins in Ancestral Contexts of Breastfeeding and Multiple Caregiving

Sybil L. Hart
Texas Tech University

THE EVOLUTION INSTITUTE

CAMBRIDGE
UNIVERSITY PRESS

Shaftesbury Road, Cambridge CB2 8EA, United Kingdom

One Liberty Plaza, 20th Floor, New York, NY 10006, USA

477 Williamstown Road, Port Melbourne, VIC 3207, Australia

314–321, 3rd Floor, Plot 3, Splendor Forum, Jasola District Centre, New Delhi – 110025, India

103 Penang Road, #05–06/07, Visioncrest Commercial, Singapore 238467

Cambridge University Press is part of Cambridge University Press & Assessment, a department of the University of Cambridge.

We share the University's mission to contribute to society through the pursuit of education, learning and research at the highest international levels of excellence.

www.cambridge.org
Information on this title: www.cambridge.org/9781009486590

DOI: 10.1017/9781009371957

© Sybil L. Hart 2024

This publication is in copyright. Subject to statutory exception and to the provisions of relevant collective licensing agreements, no reproduction of any part may take place without the written permission of Cambridge University Press & Assessment.

When citing this work, please include a reference to the DOI 10.1017/9781009371957

First published 2024

A catalogue record for this publication is available from the British Library.

ISBN 978-1-009-48659-0 Hardback
ISBN 978-1-009-37191-9 Paperback
ISSN 2752-9428 (online)
ISSN 2752-941X (print)

Cambridge University Press & Assessment has no responsibility for the persistence or accuracy of URLs for external or third-party internet websites referred to in this publication and does not guarantee that any content on such websites is, or will remain, accurate or appropriate.

Attachment and Parent-Offspring Conflict

Origins in Ancestral Contexts of Breastfeeding and Multiple Caregiving

Elements in Applied Evolutionary Science

DOI: 10.1017/9781009371957
First published online: January 2024

Sybil L. Hart
Texas Tech University
Author for correspondence: Sybil L. Hart, sybil.hart@ttu.edu

Abstract: This Element builds on the mainstream theory of attachment and contemporary understanding of the environment of evolutionary adaptedness to address the origin and nature of infant-maternal bond formation. Sections 2 and 3 propose that attachment behaviors for protesting against separation and usurpation were compelled by infants' needs for close and undivided access to a source of breast milk, usually mothers, for three years to counter threats of undernutrition and disease that were the leading causes of infant mortality. Since these attachment behaviors would not have been presented unless they were compelled by maternal resistance, their arising is also attributed to parent-offspring conflict. Section 4 theorizes that the affectional nature of infant-maternal attachment originated within contexts of breastfeeding. Uniform and universal features of exclusive *versus* complementary breastfeeding, that could entail diverse experiences among multiple caregivers, may have shaped adaptations so that love relationships with mothers differ from those with nonmaternal caregivers.

Keywords: Attachment behavior, Breast milk, Cooperative childrearing, Kwashiorkor, Lactation-based cohesion

© Sybil L. Hart 2024

ISBNs: 9781009486590 (HB), 9781009371919 (PB), 9781009371957 (OC)
ISSNs: 2752-9428 (online), 2752-941X (print)

Contents

1 Introduction

Contemporary understanding of the bond between infants and primary caregivers was revolutionized by the evolutionary theory of attachment proposed by Bowlby (1969/1982, 1973, 1980). Psychanalytic theory was still prominent when he turned to evolutionary theory and the idea that as a universal phenomenon, the infant-maternal relationship could be unraveled, like other species-typical phenomena, by entertaining the contribution of an evolved mechanism. He reasoned that the inevitability of mother-infant bond formation spoke to the possibility that it rested on some type of inherited mechanism that was forged during prehistory in the environment of evolutionary adaptedness (EEA).

In collaboration with Mary Ainsworth, Bowlby generated the mainstream theory of attachment in which it is construed as an affectional bond, the essence of which comes through Ainsworth's point that "attachment is a synonym of love" (1969, p. 1015). He is also credited for a breakthrough in terms of methodology by introducing a novel approach that draws on empirical evidence in the form of observable behavior for addressing a construct as intangible as love. This led to his focus on a class of behaviors that he referred to as the *attachment behavioral system*, by which an infant seeks proximal contact with a primary caregiver. He theorized that the regularity of contact-seeking behavior was attributable to an innately based mechanism that had been shaped under ancestral conditions where they were compelled by situations that represented potential for harm.

Bowlby recognized that such potential could have been indicated by hazards, such as physical discomfort and uncertainty over a caregiver's whereabouts. However, reports by ethologists influenced his view "that attachment behavior is always elicited at intensity in situations of alarm, which are commonly situations when a predator is either sensed or suspected. No other theory fits the facts" (Bowlby, 1969/1982, p. 226), which formed the basis of his emphasis on *cues to danger* and his impression that in the EEA these cues pertained to predation. This formulation was key to his conclusion that "protection from predators is by far the most likely function of attachment behavior" (Bowlby, 1969/1982, p. 226) and his central thesis that the infant's tendency to form attachment relationships with primary caregivers is rooted in the adaptive value of behavior that promoted proximal contact with those who are able and willing to serve as stable and predictable sources of safety and security (Ainsworth, 1969, 1972; Bowlby, 1969/1982, 1973, 1980; Feeny & Woodhouse, 2016; Mikulincer & Shaver, 2019).

Bowlby's work was conceived in terms of a basic tenet of evolutionary psychology – the premise that humans are endowed with evolved characteristics that arose as a function of evolutionary pressures, which were the forces responsible for the probability that a particular characteristic would improve or reduce an individual's chances of reproductive success (Dawkins, 1976). In general, evolutionary psychologists have focused on evolved characteristics as they pertain to adults. More recently, theorists in the field of *evolutionary developmental psychology* point out that selection pressures operate at all stages of the human lifespan (Bjorklund, 2015; Bjorklund & Blasi, 2015; Ellis & Bjorklund, 2005; Geary & Bjorklund, 2000). Even though reproductive success calls on behavior that is not available until puberty, the possibility that an individual will actually reach that point depends on whether the individual was able to withstand selection pressures that operated earlier in ontogeny, including some with starting points as early as infancy.

For example, young infants acquire fear of snakes with exceptional ease, and they do so despite never having had experience, let alone harmful experience, that involves contact with snakes (Lobue & Rakison, 2013; Rakison, 2022; Rakison & Derringer, 2008). To account for this phenomenon, there is thought that exposure to snakes was a recurrent event in the EEA where it came to represent an evolutionarily relevant stimulus due to having been a significant source of harm. The idea is not that infants are innately endowed with fear of snakes, nor that it was necessary for every ancestral infant to have been harmed by snakes. Rather, deadly encounters with snakes are seen as having occurred with sufficient regularity across the EEA, and evolutionary pressures favored infants who were psychologically prepared to acquire fear of snakes and able to display effective strategies for managing encounters with snakes.

Snakes would have been only one among any number of evolutionarily relevant stimuli in the EEA, for this was an environment that was characterized by diverse physical and social conditions, across a wide-ranging collective of periods during prehistory (Hagan & Symons, 2007; Kaplan & Robson, 2002; Silk, 2007; Wang et al., 2006). The time frame is dominated by the 2.5 million years of the Paleolithic era that was inhabited by the genus *Homo* (Scanes, 2018; Toobey & Cosmides, 1992), and includes the Pleistocene epoch, starting approximately 300,000 years ago, when modern *Homo sapiens* arose on the African continent (Armitage et al., 2011; Galway-Witham & Stringer, 2018; Osborne et al., 2008). It is also construed as encompassing dramatically different geographical conditions (Hagan & Symons, 2007; Silk, 2007). Out-migration from Africa commenced as early as 150,000 years ago (Beyer et al., 2021; Groucutt et al., 2015), and by approximately 30,000 years ago, dispersion extended as far north as Siberia. Between 14,000 and 26,000 years ago, *Homo sapiens* are believed to have reached North America via the Bering

Land Bridge and populated every continent except Antarctica (Groucutt et al., 2015; Kardulias, 2018; Praetorius et al., 2023).

The EEA was also characterized by social conditions that could exert evolutionary pressures. Throughout the majority of our evolutionary history, *Homo sapiens* lived as nomadic hunter-gatherers in sparsely populated clans (Eibl-Eibesfeldt, 1989; Narvaez et al., 2014) that have often been construed as typified by the !Kung, one of the San-speaking peoples of Botswana that has been studied for insight into the hunting and gathering way of life. In this traditional society, child rearing has been described as involving intense contact between mothers and infants over extended periods of time (Lee, 1976). For Bowlby, this description aligned with ethologists' reports of behavior by primates, as well as the consistent care and continuous contact model of maternal caregiving that was customary in Western settings. So, when he rejected psychoanalytic traditions that emphasized intrapsychic structures in the form of the id, ego, and superego, he did so in favor of interpersonal mechanisms, with emphasis was on the infant's relationship with a "mother-figure."

The figure that received the preponderance of attention was the biological mother since at the time and place of Bowlby's work, mothers were the most likely sources of stable and predictable care, and for the next half-century, the mother–child dyad became the main unit of attachment theorists' investigations. However, starting as early as the 1920s, field studies across a range of non-Western localities, such as Margaret Mead's work in Bali, Samoa, and New Guinea, yielded evidence which suggested that throughout most of evolutionary history, mother–infant dyads were embedded within dense social networks whose members contributed to inclusive fitness through activities that included nonmaternal, also known as allomaternal, care of the young (Burkart et al., 2009; Gurven, 2004; Hill et al., 2011; Silk, 2006). Cooperative child rearing has been documented in contemporary societies where it has been found associated with increases in maternal reproductive success and offspring survival (Hrdy, 2009; Konner, 2018).

The networks are also responsible for creating a social milieu that provides infants with opportunities to associate with caregivers other than mothers. Because the construct of attachment is not easily quantified, especially when it is applied outside Western settings, it is unclear whether and how any of these infant–caregiver relationships can be characterized as affectional bonds, consistent with the construct of attachment (Meehan & Hawks, 2014). Nevertheless, there is thought that through repeated interactions with nonmaternal caregivers who respond with promptness and warmth, infants can form trusting internal models of a relatively small subset of caregivers, thereby cultivating bonds that appear to align with the construct of attachment

(Ainsworth, 1967; Howes & Spieker, 2008; Tronick et al., 1992; van IJzendoorn et al., 1992). Potential for attachment relationships with nonmaternal caregivers raises questions that pertain to the elevated status of the infant-maternal relationship. Its omnipresence is apparent even in non-Western cultures where allomaternal investment is extensive (Hrdy, 2009; Meehan & Hawks, 2014) and is well known to occur among nonhuman primates. As Hrdy pointed out "of all the attachments mammalian babies form, none is more powerful than that between baby primates and their mothers" (Hrdy, 2009, p. 68). Indeed, it is the case that among humans, the infant-maternal relationship is the only infant–caregiver relationship that is recognized as a universal phenomenon (Hart, 2022a).

The goal of this Element is to shed fresh light on the infant-maternal relationship through attention to the bond that infants form with their mothers. Our approach centers on its evolved foundation and the basis of its omnipresence, as well as mechanisms that shaped its affective nature so as to have arisen as an affectional bond. Each of the next three sections builds on a central concept of the mainstream theory of attachment (Bowlby, 1969/1982) through treatment that is informed by contemporary understanding of physical and ecological features of the EEA as the context for which our genotype is selected. Throughout this Element, our focus is on infants up to 36 months of age, with those in the 13- to 36-month age range at times referred to as toddlers. The 36-month age range brackets the period that attachment theorists consider necessary for a bond of attachment to become fully formed (Ainsworth, 1964; Ainsworth et al., 1972, 1978; Bowlby, 1969/1982). It also aligns with advocacy by public health organizations, such as Zero-to-Three (Zero-to-Three, 2022), that identify it as a discrete stage on the basis of entailing exceptionally rapid postnatal brain growth (Bjorklund, 2022; Hrvoj-Mihic et al., 2013; Locke & Bogin, 2022; Wilder & Semendeferi, 2022).

Section 2, Evolutionary Pressures during the First 1,000 Days of Life in the Environment of Evolutionary Adaptedness (EEA), follows from Bowlby's insight into attachment formation as an adaptation that arose from evolutionary pressures stemming from influences that posed mortal threat to infants. Various sources of influence are tapped to identify a recurrent, species-typical event that is likely to have been responsible for infant mortality in the EEA. This leads to discussing the likelihood of harm in the form of morbidity, and how vulnerability to disease is likely to have been exacerbated by risks associated with undernutrition due to premature weaning upon the closely spaced birth of a sibling. These vulnerabilities are addressed further in Section 3, The Attachment Behavioral System and Parent–Offspring Conflict, through attention to their role in the origination of two components of the attachment behavioral system, *separation protest* and *jealousy protest*. These negatively valenced presentations are discussed in terms of their moderating effects on vulnerability to morbidity, their adaptiveness in the context of parent–offspring conflict, and their contribution to the infant-maternal relationship arising as a species-wide phenomenon.

Section 4, The Affectional Nature of Attachment, turns to addressing positive emotionality that characterizes infants' bonds with mothers, and how it could have been shaped by ancestral conditions. Following attachment theorists' highlighting the importance of contextual influences, this section addresses the dynamics of breastfeeding in the EEA. Distinct stages of breastfeeding behaviors are identified on the basis of maturational and bio-behavioral features of infants, and discussed in terms of implications toward defining forums for social interactions with maternal and nonmaternal caregivers, each with potential to correspond with different kinds of experiences that could have shaped expectations, psychological adaptations, and relationships. Section 5, Applications, concludes by touching on topics that pertain to lactation and attachment formation in contemporary settings, and recommendations for addressing toddler-aged infants' adjustment upon the birth of a sibling.

2 Evolutionary Pressures during the First 1,000 Days of Life

In line with mainstream concepts of attachment formation as the outcome of adaptations that were compelled by threat to ancestral infants' survival, this section draws on contemporary understanding of that environment to identify a recurrent, species-typical event that could have been responsible for infant mortality.

2.1 Infant Mortality

During the 2.5 million years prior to the Holocene, the current geological epoch that began approximately 11,000 years ago with the advent of agriculture and pastoralism, population growth is thought to have increased at a rate of less than 1 percent per year. Because fertility during this period is believed to have ranged from approximately 4 to 8 children per woman, with an average that is estimated between 4.1 and 5.4 (Hawks et al., 2000; Kramer, 2019; White, 2014), the slow rate of population growth during the Pleistocene epoch is not usually attributed to low rates of fecundity. Rather, it is attributed to staggeringly high rates of mortality (Bocquet-Appel, 2011; White, 2014). Estimates based on rates of fertility and longevity have led to suggestion that of 4.1 offspring born to Pleistocene women, only 2.3 survived (Kramer, 2019).

Death rates were not evenly distributed across age groups. Due to limitations in the availability of paleodemographic archeological data on ancestral hunter-gatherers, their modern counterparts are often tapped as a proxy. In addition to being genetically similar to their ancestral analogues, modern hunter-gatherers function comparably in terms of lifestyle, and so they are thought to be comparable in terms of population demographics. To derive an estimate of the mortality profile across age, Volk et al. (McDowell & Volk, 2022; Volk & Atkinson, 2008, 2013) conducted analyses on populations of extant hunter-gatherers with sufficiently large sample sizes and minimal contact with modern resources that impact mortality. Findings revealed that mortality rates of children up to 15 years of age ranged from 22 percent among the Efé, part-time hunter-gatherers living in the Ituri Rainforest of the Democratic Republic of Congo, to 56 percent among the Mbuti, another indigenous group that inhabits the Ituri Rainforest Congo region in Africa. This yielded an average child mortality rate of approximately 49 percent.

The data also shed light on the mortality rates of extant hunter-gatherer infants up to 12 months of age. These were found ranging from 14 percent among the Efé, to 40.5 percent among the Semang, a group living in forest regions of Malaysia, yielding an average mortality rate of 26.8 percent (McDowell & Volk, 2022; Volk & Atkinson, 2008, 2013). Estimates of the mortality rate of infants up to the age of 3 years can be inferred from an analysis of ethnographic data on extant hunter-gatherers by White (2014). According to his analyses, the chance of death among 12- to 24-month-olds was as great as that of infants in the first year. Mortality rates of infants in the third year were almost as great.

A similar pattern that highlighted increased risk of mortality in infants up to 3 years of age emerged from work that drew from osteoarcheological methodology. Excavation of several archaeological sites in Argentina yielded a sample of human skeletons that consisted of several thousand bones (Flensborg et al., 2015). Paleodemographic estimates of age at the time of death were determined through analyses of teeth and bone tissue as well as measurements of long bone length (Boldsen et al., 2022; Buikstra & Konigsberg, 1985). Findings revealed that the remains were of ancestral hunter-gatherer individuals of all ages, a preponderance of whom were older adults with life spans as long as 72 years (Pontzer et al., 2018) and infants up to the age of 3 years. This generated a bimodal pattern suggesting a mortality profile marked by two peaks, one made up of infants up to 3 years of age and a second one that did not appear until adulthood (Flensborg et al., 2015).

2.2 Causes of Infant Mortality in the EEA

The nature of pressures that were responsible for infant mortality can be unraveled through attention to a sequence of events that culminated in death. Findings on extant hunter-gatherers as well as acculturated extant hunter-gatherers suggest that 75 percent of deaths among children up to 15 years of age are due to disease. Among infants up to the age of 12 months of age, infectious and gastrointestinal disease, particularly pneumonia and diarrhea, are the most frequent causes of death (Gurven & Kaplan, 2007; McDowell & Volk, 2022).

Insight into the outsized influence of illness on infant mortality can be unearthed from the body of literature on causes of death among contemporary populations who live in nonindustrialized countries, mostly in low-resource regions of Asia and Africa (Warr, 2014). These groups do not live the lifestyle of hunter-gathers and so caution is warranted in drawing analogies with ancestral counterparts, yet they are characterized by mortality profiles that show some parallels with those of ancestral hunter-gatherers. In 2003, over 10 million children under the age of 5 years died (Black et al., 2003; Ramani et al., 2010). These data include findings on children in Ethiopia and Myanmar (Dadi, 2015; Hoehn & Hoppenz, 2009), where one out of eleven children died before their fifth birthday. These statistics lead to suggestion that the under-five mortality rate (U5MR) is almost as great as that of extant hunter-gatherer infants, such as the Efé (Volk & Atkinson, 2013), especially when considering that the rate is thought to be an underestimate of death rates at times and in places marked by extreme poverty and conflict.

Furthermore, the U5MR in these countries exceeds the mortality rate of any other age group until late adulthood (Christian, 2008; de Onis, 2008), suggesting a bimodal mortality profile across age with an initial peak during infancy/ early childhood that mirrors findings on past and contemporary hunter-gatherers (Flensborg et al., 2015; White, 2014). Also, reminiscent of osteoarcheological findings on ancestral hunter-gatherers (Flensborg et al., 2015) and in line with findings on extant hunter-gatherer infants (White, 2014), there is evidence which suggests that the U5MR is driven by high rates of mortality that extend beyond the first year. Early epidemiological studies (Dyson, 1977) noted that mortality rates of infants in the 12- to 24-month age range were as great as those of infants in the first year. More recently, interventions are being designed with the aim of targeting infants up to 24 months of age, a focus that is designed in light of evidence that exceptionally high risk of mortality extends through the second year (Lamberti et al., 2013; Narayan et al., 2019; Ubesie et al., 2012).

Literature on the U5MR reveals that half of the children with the highest U5MRs live in six countries where the leading causes of death in the first year are associated with perinatal conditions, such as prematurity, intrauterine growth restriction, and low birth weight that usually affect infants within the first 6 months of life (Hoehn & Hoppenz, 2009; Ramani et al., 2010; Ray, 2011). As infants enter the second year of life, the leading causes of mortality are not unlike those affecting their ancestral counterparts, that is, infectious and gastrointestinal diseases, mostly pneumonia and diarrheal diseases (Andegiorgish et al., 2022; Black et al., 2003; Liu et al., 2015; Ramani et al., 2010; Saloojee & Pettifor, 2005; Troeger et al., 2018).

Causes of infant mortality other than disease have received less attention, though a few studies reported on incidences due to accidents. Reports from India and Asia indicate that accidents which involve infants are usually caused by falls and are not fatal. Those that are fatal account for 1.4 percent of deaths among infants under 1 year, 8 percent of deaths among 1- to 5-year-olds, and 57 percent of deaths among 5- to 17-year-olds, primarily due to drowning (Hss et al., 2014; Linnan et al., 2007; Ramani et al., 2010). As in analyses on mortality due to disease, epidemiological data on infants are not treated separately from those on children up to 5 years of age. Nevertheless, it seems reasonable to conclude that the EEA was a setting where fatalities due to accidents occurred at low rates during the first 3 years. Predation and environmental hazards would have occurred in the EEA, and it is likely that they were responsible for adaptations that were relevant to inclusive fitness (Barrett, 2015; Duntley, 2015). However, scant evidence points to these hazards as having occurred at rates that could have been responsible for evolutionary pressures that gave rise to adaptations in infants.

2.3 Risk Factors: Undernutrition and Close Birth Spacing

Undernutrition is likely to have featured in the EEA, and recent reports on contemporary hunter-gatherers by medical and nutritional anthropologists suggest that even intermittent exposure is likely to have had disproportionate effects on infants (Bogin, 2011; De Souza, 2006). For example, anthropometric measures of !Kung children revealed that most of the 1- to 5-year-olds had height and weight measures that were below the 3rd percentile, which is a sign of stunting that usually results from long-term exposure to nutritional deprivation (WHO, 2023a). In addition, skinfold measures, that indicate effects of more immediate exposure to undernutrition (WHO, 2023a), yielded scores below the 50th percentile. This was especially apparent during the dry season when clean water and sustenance were less plentiful (Bogin, 2011; Lee, 1976; Truswell & Hansen, 1976). Despite long-held assumptions that the children's small stature was attributable to genetic influences, recent studies that include comparisons with genetically similar samples of neighboring pastoralists fail to support that impression. Thus, some combination of long-term exposure to suboptimal nutrition and acute phases of food scarcity are thought to have accounted for mortality rates of !Kung children that were reported to have been as great as 45 percent (Bogin, 2011; De Souza, 2006).

Contemporary hunter-gatherers face conditions that are not identical to those in the ancestral past (Crittenden & Schnorr, 2017; Zucoloto, 2011). However, transient substandard diet and its roots in food scarcity (Bekele et al., 2020) are thought to have exerted some degree of pressure on ancestral peoples since their nomadic lifestyle and eventual migration out of Africa, which reached areas as harsh and remote as Siberia, were directly or indirectly driven by the quest for sustenance under conditions that varied with seasonality and unpredictable resources (Burke et al., 2017; Mannino et al., 2011; Zhu et al., 2021). Given modern humans' genetic similarity with our ancestral analogues, the consequences of undernutrition, such as the disproportionate effects on infants, are likely to resemble those which are evident in present-day settings.

An immense body of epidemiological literature (Alberda et al., 2006; Bhutta et al., 2017; Black et al., 2003; Ray, 2011; Worthman, 2014) as well as numerous public health organizations, including UNICEF's State of the World's Children report (2019), have been unequivocal in reporting that of the millions of young children who die each year in under-resourced areas, the main underlying cause is undernutrition. In these cases, undernutrition is indicated by anthropometric signs of protein-energy malnutrition (PEM): stunting, wasting, and underweight, which is a medical classification that uses weight-for-age ratios to derive cutoffs, such as the WHO Child Growth Standard of <2 standard deviations (WHO, 2023a), to identify affected infants and children because weight-for-height measures, such as body mass index (BMI), are inaccurate in settings where stunting is prevalent.

These signs of undernutrition tend to coincide with one of the PEM diseases, marasmus and kwashiorkor. Marasmus is caused by overall calorie depletion that amounts to starvation. It is diagnosed by visible signs of wasting, coupled with weakness and lethargy as the body conserves energy. Upon further deterioration, the body begins to feed on its own tissues, and organ failure ensues. In contrast with marasmus, which is attributed to deficiency of all macronutrients, that is, protein, carbohydrates and fats, kwashiorkor results from inadequate protein intake. It can occur even if the total calorie intake is not insufficient if the diet is high in carbohydrates but low in protein, as in diets where maize is the primary source of nutrition. The most recognizable sign of kwashiorkor is the distended abdomen, which is often accompanied by emaciated limbs and behavior suggesting irritability (Bahwal et al., 2020; Guyatt et al., 2020; Ray, 2011; Seaman, 1972).

Symptoms of both of the PEM diseases include compromised immune function as well as digestive system impairments that limit the capacity for nutrient absorption even when nutrition becomes available. Consequently, afflicted individuals are more prone to infection and less responsive to treatment. This exacerbates vulnerability to the increased metabolic demands of diseases with etiologies that are unrelated to undernutrition, so that comorbidities frequently occur. Children suffering from severe acute malnutrition are nearly twelve times more likely to die from diseases, such as respiratory and parasitic infections, malaria, and measles, that would not have been fatal were it not for complications due to poor nutrition (Bahwal et al., 2020; Benjamin & Lappin, 2021; Kassaw et al., 2021; Narayan et al., 2019; Seaman, 1972).

In such cases, one of the strongest predictors of mortality is being within the 9- to 24-month age range (Guyatt et al., 2020). For example, a recent case-controlled study of hospitalized infants and children in Yemen found that the risk of PEM disease was greatest among infants in the 6- to 24-month age range, most of whom were also suffering from diarrhea and pneumonia (Bahwal et al., 2020). These findings highlight the point that at no time in an individual's life is nutrition of greater importance than during the first 1,000 days of life, which is the time span between conception and the infant's second birthday. As the period that is associated with greatest potential for optimal health and development, it is also characterized by the exceptional degree to which infants are vulnerable to disease (UNICEF, 2023;Thousaddays.org, 2023).

Inquiry into undernutrition as the basis of vulnerability to disease among children in this age range has been addressed in an abundant body of literature that has consistently pointed to the importance of breast milk (Briend et al., 1988; Clavano, 1982; Feachem & Koblinsky, 1984; Hoyle et al., 1980; Huffman & Combest, 1990; Victora et al., 1987; Worthman, 2014). These studies have identified nutrients, such as proteins that are necessary for energy, as well as bioactive factors that defend infant health and growth by offering protection against inflammation and infection while supporting immune maturation, organ development, and healthy microbial colonization (Ballard & Morrow, 2013; Grammatikaki & Huybrechts, 2016; Hinde & Milligan, 2011). Findings on the immunological, hormonal, and nutritional components of human milk that are responsible for its protective effects spurred the promotion of breastfeeding as a cornerstone of international efforts to address the U5MR, such as the United Nations Millennium Development Goal (United Nations, 2015) of lowering the rate of infant mortality from its peak level in 1990 (Alderman & Fernald, 2017; Black et al., 2015; John et al., 2017; Prado & Dewey, 2014). These organizations recommend breastfeeding for 24 months, along with complementary foods starting no earlier than six months (CDC, 2023a, 2023b; Meek & Noble, 2022; WHO, 2023b).

In light of the importance of breast milk to infant health, it is not surprising that there are few reports of ancestral infants being fully weaned prior to the age of 30 months. Based on isotopic studies of teeth and bone tissue, ancestral hunter-gatherers are thought to have breastfed for approximately 42 months (Clayton et al., 2006; Eerkens & Bartelink, 2013; Loponte & Mazza, 2021; Tessone et al., 2015; Waters-Rist et al., 2011), though the timing of this transition would have differed with cultural traditions and the availability of soft foods (Dettwyler, 1995; Kimminau, 2021). Among extant hunter-gatherer societies, weaning concludes by approximately 29 months (Veile & Miller, 2021). However, breastfeeding tends to conclude earlier in cases that involve a closely spaced subsequent pregnancy (Bøhler & Bergström, 1995a; Molitoris, 2019) where it is compelled by its energetic costs. Lactation is the costliest aspect of human reproduction. In fact, the calorie requirements of lactation actually exceed those of gestation (Hinde & Milligan, 2011; Quinn, 2016). Whereas pregnant women require approximately 400 supplemental kilocalories per day, lactating women require approximately 500–600 supplemental kilocalories per day (Kominiarek & Rajan, 2016; Kramer, 2019), and these requirements are even greater for women who breastfeed while pregnant. In these instances, 500–650 supplemental kilocalories per day are needed to support lactation, plus 400 supplemental kilocalories per day to support gestation for a total of approximately 900–1050 supplemental kilocalories per day (American Pregnancy Association, 2023). These estimates are based on populations of well-nourished women, whose daily intakes involve approximately 2,000 kilocalories per day, resulting in a total daily requirement for approximately 3,000 kilocalories. For women who are undernourished, the requirements are thought to be even greater (Girma et al., 2022; Kominiarek & Rajan, 2016; Udipi, 2000).

Conditions where the calorie requirements of pregnant women are unmet contribute to maternal depletion that poses heightened risks to women and newborn infants (Bauserman et al., 2020; Girma et al., 2022; Udipi et al., 2000; Yaya et al., 2020). These risks are increased by inter-pregnancy intervals (IPIs) of short duration and increased still further by concurrent lactation (López-Fernández et al., 2017). Pregnancy-lactation overlap has been associated with maternal anemia, cesarean delivery, prolonged labor, intrauterine growth restriction, and low birth weight. Some evidence points to increased risk of prematurity and miscarriage (Molitoris, 2019; Sengül et al., 2013; Shaaban et al., 2015) as well as growth delays and stunting among the newborn infants (Guyatt et al., 2020).

It seems likely that customs which prohibit women from breastfeeding during pregnancy (Lancy, 2008; Shostak, 1976) grew from appreciating the risks of pregnancy-lactation overlap (Dewey & Cohen, 2007; Dufour & Sauther, 2002). For ancestral women, close birth-spacing would have been an atypical event, but it could not have been unknown. Since women gave birth as many as 8 times (Hawks et al., 2000; White, 2014), and did so in the absence of modern methods of birth control, birth spacing could not have been planned so that each inter-birth interval (IBI) could last as long as 4 years. In cases where IBIs were less than 4 years, IPIs would have been less than 27 months, and so mothers of toddlers would have been confronted by the overlapping energetic demands of a toddler-aged nursling and a fetus.

Unfortunately, limiting lactation during a closely spaced subsequent pregnancy meant that toddler-aged nurslings were subjected to early weaning, and evidence suggests that the benefits to pregnant women and neonates come at costs to existing toddlers. Studies conducted in Bhutan, Ethiopia, Bangladesh, and Guinea-Bissau show that in under-resourced regions, a closely spaced subsequent pregnancy has been associated with early weaning of existing toddlers who showed signs of compromised nutritional status (Bøhler & Bergström, 1995b; 1996; Bøhler et al., 1995; Hailemariam & Tesfaye, 1997; Jakobsen et al., 2003; Koenig et al., 1990; Mozumder et al., 2000; Rahman et al., 1996), as well as heightened risk of mortality. For example, work conducted in Senegal found that mortality rates were quadrupled among 2-year-olds whose mothers had already given birth to a sibling (Ronsmans, 1996). Research in Kenya found that mortality rates were doubled among toddlers who had encountered a sibling's birth by the time they reached 20 months of age (Fotso et al., 2013).

Tragically, toddler-aged weanlings succumb to one of the protein-energy malnutrition diseases, and apparently, this eventuality is not unfamiliar. Kwashiorkor takes its name from a term native to Ghana that literally means "the disease the deposed baby gets when the next one is born" (Williams et al., 1935, p. 1151). The condition is also known as "the sickness of weaning" (Batool et al., 2015), language that again implies longstanding awareness, not merely with visible signs of the disease, such as abdominal swelling, but also with the circumstances responsible for their presentation. Perhaps due to their grasp of the risks to toddlers, pregnant mothers of toddler-aged nurslings often slacken the pace of weaning during pregnancy, and so some amount of breast-feeding during pregnancy is not uncommon despite its energetic cost.

Upon parturition, however, the energetic cost of tandem breastfeeding of two energetically dependent offspring would become even more apparent, which has contributed to customs where the birth of twins or the existence of an unweaned toddler have been cause for divestment, either through abandonment or infanticide (Hrdy, 1994; Scrimshaw, 1984). An alternative, and less drastic, option for reducing the energetic cost of investment in two nurslings involves allomaternal breastfeeding. However, the practice of wet nursing among extant hunter-gatherer women is not normative (Hewlett & Winn, 2014) and tends to be limited to situations where it has been compelled by motherlessness due to maternal illness or mortality (Ainsworth, 1967; Frimpong-Nnuroh, 2004; Williams et al., 1935).

Barriers to allomaternal breastfeeding involve several types of obstacles. One stems from the fact that it requires that a lactating woman distribute her own infant's supply of breast milk for the benefit of nonbiological offspring. Given the energetic cost of tandem breastfeeding, undertaking it in areas where food insecurity is prevalent comes at a cost to the wet-nurse's biological offspring, which is a cost that is usually found unacceptable (Hrdy, 2007). In most cases, lactating women who are childless, usually as a consequence of their own infants' mortality, are the most likely alternative sources of breast milk since biological offspring are not imperiled (Dettwyler, 1995; Humphrey, 2010; Stuart-Macadam, 1995). In the EEA, however, these women were scarce, especially since hunter-gatherer societies were thinly populated clans, rarely consisting of more than fifty persons including children (Eibl-Eibesfeldt, 1989; Narvaez et al., 2014).

It was not until the Holocene, when villages arose, that allomaternal breast-feeding became more feasible. Greater population density led to increases in the available pool of potential wet nurses. At the same time, pastoralism yielded alternative sources of milk, while agriculture yielded complementary foods soft enough to be consumed by infants (Bocquet-Appel, 2011; Williams (1933); Dettwyler, 1995; Ellison, 1995; Howcroft et al., 2012). Thus, it seems likely that in most cases, allomaternal support involved cooperative acts such as those that have been documented in extant hunter-gatherer societies (Henry & Morelli, 2022; Hrdy, 1994; Kramer, 2019) where pregnant and lactating women have been found able to increase their intake of calories and reduce their energetic expenditure through the support of allomaternal assistants who share provisions and substitute for the mother's labor (Henry & Morelli, 2022; Kramer, 2019).

In rare instances, a mother could have been substituted by a non-lactating foster mother, usually the grandmother. In modern Western settings, lactation can be induced following a process that involves the foster mother's early and regular use of a breast pump and the administration of hormones. Even with their use, milk supplies are often delayed and inadequate. Outside modern Western settings, success would have depended on an infant, ideally a full-term neonate with a well-developed sucking reflex, able to withstand hunger until lactogenesis was induced, something that can take several weeks (Bryant, 2006; Lawrence, 2022; Shannon et al., 2008). In the context of food insecurity, it is still the case that allomaternal breastfeeding and induced lactation are challenging, if not futile, as illustrated in an account by Williams (1933). She was the physician who is credited with having diagnosed the causative agent and identified the remedy for kwashiorkor, work for which she received numerous honors and was appointed the first director of the Mother and Child Health (MCH) section of the World Health Organization (WHO). Based on her observations while living and working among Ghanian women during the early1930s, she wrote,

> Kwashiorkor is usually observed between the ages of six months and four years ... among patients at the Children's Hospital, Accra, the mortality being about 90 percent. The history always includes defective feeding. The mother is sick, old, and malnourished, or has become pregnant again while the patient is still very young. (Williams et al., 1935, p. 1151)

> The surviving baby is generally adopted by the maternal grandmother, and breast-fed by her possibly with the help of her sisters and other daughters. The women of a family often live in a compound together, so the arrangement is simple. These foster-children generally die early. (Williams, 1933, pp. 912–551)

In sum, flat population growth during the 2.5 million years of the Pleistocene epoch has been attributed to rates of child mortality that were as great as 49 percent, and evidence suggests that most cases occurred during the first 3 years of life. Based on ethnographic studies of extant hunter-gatherers, paleo-demographic archeological data on ancestral hunter-gatherers, and epidemiological reports on contemporary populations in low-resource regions with parallel mortality profiles, the greatest threat to infant mortality in the EEA is likely to have been morbidity. The infants who were most likely to succumb to disease were those who had been subjected to weaning prior to the age of 30 months. This would have occurred in instances where interbirth intervals were less than 4 years, which was atypical but likely to have been a recurrent event given the absence of modern methods of birth control. Early weaning that was necessary to avert pregnancy-lactation overlap which posed risk to birth outcomes had serious consequences for existing ancestral toddlers. Deprived of mothers' milk and without an alternative source, they would have been left without its protective effects while still at ages when they depended on it for nutrition and passive resistance to disease.

3 The Attachment Behavioral System and Parent–Offspring Conflict

The premise that infant mortality in the EEA was primarily due to morbidity leads to conjecture that evolutionary pressures would have favored infants who sought care, not from caregivers as sources of safety and protection against predation and environmental dangers (Bowlby, 1969/1982), but rather from mothers as sources of breast milk for protection against disease. Thus, we turn to the attachment behavioral system, the class of evolved behaviors for seeking care, to explore whether and how some of its features could have been compelled by infant reliance on mothers' milk, and how these features could have played a role in shaping infant attachment to mother.

3.1 Separation Protest

By approaching the construct of attachment through attention to observable behavior, Bowlby noted the infant's "tendency not to let mother out of sight or earshot, which is readily observed in human infants during the latter half of their first year and throughout their second and third years of life" (Bowlby, 1958; p. 40). This pattern was also reported by Ainsworth during fieldwork in Uganda, where she observed protest behavior upon the mother's departure by infants, starting at the age of 6 to 7 months (Ainsworth, 1964), that has since been documented in a number of forger societies (Meehan & Hawk, 2014). For Bowlby, these observations underscored the significance of close contact between infants and mothers that had been noted in a number of prominent early reports (Bowlby, 1953; Bowlby et al., 1952; Freud & Dann, 1951; Heinicke, 1956) that documented acute breakdown in infants' cognitive, psychosocial, and somatic functioning when close contact was disrupted by separation. In conjunction with his clinical experience, these reports inspired Bowlby's interest in *separation distress*, the negatively valenced behaviors that infants demonstrate when faced with a primary caregiver's absence.

This phenomenon, later referred to as *separation protest*, was explored in classic work by Kagan (1976), Kagan et al. (1980), and Kearsley et al. (1975) on infants' responses during exposure to their mother's departure. He found that when infants were exposed to this event, they responded by crying, but this was not apparent until infants reached the age of 9 months. After its onset, crying increased and peaked at 18 months. By the second birthday it began to decline and continued to do so until the third birthday. The inverted arc, with its peak at 18 months, was perplexing given that earlier findings on the age profile associated with crying showed that its peak occurs much earlier, during the first three months, and is followed by steady decline so that by 9 months crying is reduced to a low level that remains flat throughout infancy (Baildam et al., 1995; Emde et al., 1976). This profile was also found to be characteristic of !Kung infants (Barr et al., 1991). Thus, it seemed unlikely that separation protest, with its peak at 18 months, could be explained by influences associated with maturation.

The readiness with which crying was expressed by infants upon mothers' departure, and its presentation even in the absence of harm or history of experiencing harm in such instances, led Kagan to entertain the contribution of an innately based foundation. He explored that possibility and whether it differed with history of exposure to maternal absence by conducting cross-cultural studies that included infants from backgrounds where multiple care-giving was normative. The samples included Ladino and Mayan Guatemalans, !Kung San infants of Botswana, and Israeli infants who were being reared in communal settings (summarized in Kagan et al., 1980; Lester et al., 1974). Findings revealed that maternal departure precipitated crying in each sample of infants that was not apparent until late in the first year, when it was followed by a sharp increase that peaked between 12 and 16 months and was followed by a steep decline that led to resolution by 30–36 months (see Figure 1). Comparisons revealed commonality across cultures which led to consensus that separation protest is a species-typical characteristic of infants in the second year of life. This conclusion was upheld by replications (Super et al., 2012) as well by work that addressed the potential contribution of experience to infants' presentations of separation protest by drawing comparisons between infants who were home-reared *versus* those with more experience of maternal absence by having attended day care. Findings revealed that the two groups did not differ from each other (Kearsley et al., 1975).

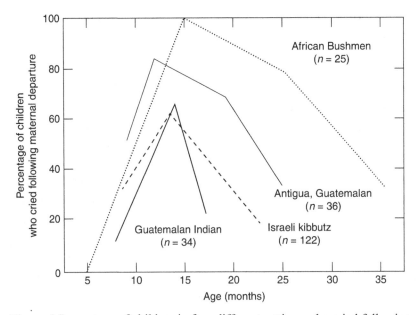

Figure 1 Percentage of children in four different settings who cried following maternal departure. Reprinted from *Infancy: Its Place in Human Development* by Jerome Kagan, Richard B. Kearsley, and Philip R. Zelazo, 1978, p. 107, with permission from the publisher, Cambridge, MA: Harvard University Press

Kagan and associates (1976) and Kagan et al., (1980) interpreted the results by proposing that by the end of the first year, cognitive development that underpins memory is responsible for distress upon maternal departure by presenting infants with a situation that they perceive as an unexpected event. By the third year, maturation of cognitive competencies allows infants to resolve uncertainty over discrepancies, such as maternal absence. Attachment theorists have incorporated the role of experience. Separation protest is seen as having onset by the end of the first year in accord with experience by which a psychological bond with a primary caregiver begins to form, peaks in the second year as infants come to fear the bond being broken, and declines in the third year as the bond is consolidated on the basis of cognitive development and experiences that yield confidence in the primary caregiver as a reliable source of support and the formation of goal-corrected partnerships (Ainsworth, 1969; Ainsworth et al., 1972, 1978; Waters et al., 1991).

In their attention to influences that stem from advances in cognition and experiences associated with socialization, these interpretations address proximate causality, meaning that the explanations pertain to events that exert immediate influence on infants in contemporary settings. However, as a phenomenon that is construed as a human universal, it is appropriate to also consider ultimate levels of causation. At this level, the events of interest are those that pertained to ancestral infants and conditions in the ancestral past that could have operated as evolutionary pressures on the process of natural selection by favoring infants with characteristics that were adaptive in that environment (Dawkins, 1976). Clues toward unraveling the inherited basis of separation protest can be approached by noting that the inverted arc, with its peak during the second year, that characterizes separation protest also characterizes the time frame that bracketed ancestral infants' vulnerability to undernutrition (Dyson, 1977; Flensborg et al., 2015; Lamberti et al., 2013; Narayan et al., 2019; Ubesie, 2012; White, 2014).

The overlap in the timing of separation protest and vulnerability to undernutrition may stem from a common origin in the EEA that involved risks to ancestral infants between the ages of 9 and 30 months. Prior to the age of 9 months, the adaptive advantages of separation protest would have been minimal given that a subsequent pregnancy would have been the sole reason for a mother to halt breastfeeding, and it was rare for a mother to have already been pregnant, and so the chance of weaning was low. This being the case, separation from mother would not have represented risk of undernutrition to degrees that compelled behavioral adaptations in the form of separation protest. In general, weaning of such young infants was unknown except in cases where it eventuated from maternal illness or death, in which case it was likely to have resulted in infant mortality (Chikhungu et al., 2017; Gracey, 2004; Masmas et al., 2004; Williams, 1933).

For children over 30 months of age, the adaptive advantage of separation protest would have also been minimal, but for a different reason. By this point, a child had survived past the first 1,000 days and as discussed earlier, the child's metabolic requirements could be satisfied without breast milk. Therefore, maternal absence would not have posed threat of undernutrition or morbidity. Indeed, this age marks the juncture when it was not uncommon for ancestral mothers to start to bring weaning to conclusion (Clayton et al., 2006; Eerkens & Bartelink, 2013; Loponte & Mazza, 2021; Tessone et al., 2015; Waters-Rist et al., 2011).

For 9- to 30-month-olds, however, maternal absence would have represented mortal threat of undernutrition, for it would have signified maternal unavailability that held potential for loss of access to mothers' milk. This situation would have been consequential by occurring precisely during the time frame when undernutrition had the greatest chance of being fatal (Bøhler & Bergström, 1995a; Molitoris, 2019; Williams, 1933; Williams et al., 1935). From this perspective, it seems plausible that encounters with maternal absence were interpreted as a potential source of harm, which prepared infants to treat maternal absence by demonstrating strategies that kept mothers from leaving. This calculation of threat level as a function of infant age leads to conceptualizing separation protest as an ontogenetic adaptation (Bjorklund, 2015; Bjorklund & Hart, 2022). As such, it can be understood as an adaptation that arose due to having been of benefit to survival strictly during a specific time frame. Once that benefit diminished, so did the behavior.

In sum, we have shown that in the EEA, where disease represented the greatest threat to infant survival, breast milk was of paramount importance to infant survival, and so we theorized that any indication of potential for its denial posed threat of harm and was so consequential that it operated as a threat-relevant cue. Our thesis is that by the age of 9 months, maternal absence represented one such cue, and it would have occurred as a recurrent, species-typical event so as to have served as an evolutionarily relevant stimulus. As a tactic for deterring maternal unavailability, separation protest would have been adaptive toward retaining the health benefits of mothers' milk, and so evolutionary pressures would have selected 9- to 30-month-olds who demonstrated this behavior. Admittedly, the evolved basis of separation protest could have been shaped by its advantage toward mitigating some other type of pressure that jeopardized infant health. However, it is difficult to identify a hazard that posed threat of morbidity, that would have been a recurrent, species-typical event across the widely different geographical conditions that humans inhabited throughout the 2.5 million years of the Paleolithic era, that targeted 1- and 2-year-olds, and declined precipitously during the third year.

3.2 Jealousy Protest

We have proposed that by deterring mothers from leaving, separation protest was adaptive toward reducing the risk of morbidity and mortality by helping to secure infant access to mothers' milk. However, the dynamics of the infant-maternal relationship would have been altered by a subsequent pregnancy and the introduction of a competitor.

Pregnancy-lactation overlap posed risks to mothers and infants, which was a predicament that could not have been unknown in the EEA. Breastfeeding during pregnancy has been observed among extant hunter-gatherer populations (Fouts et al., 2005; Gray, 1996; Lancy, 2008; McDade & Worthman, 1998; Shostak, 1976), as well as in contemporary settings marked by food insecurity (Girma et al., 2022; Humphrey, 2010; López-Fernández et al., 2017; Molitoris, 2019; Narayan et al., 2019; Udipi et al., 2000). However, upon parturition it would become clear to mothers that they could not support the energetic cost of tandem breastfeeding of two energetically dependent offspring. In the context of food insecurity, mothers of two infants, a neonate and a toddler, tend to act on the probability that weaning is more likely to be a death sentence for a neonate than a toddler, who, after all, has at least some chance of survival. Thought that ancestral mothers were similarly informed has been the basis of understanding that upon a newborn infant's arrival, toddlers' chances of having continued access to breast milk declined, and in most cases, it came to a complete halt (Dettwyler, 1995; Humphrey, 2010; Stuart-Macadam, 1995).

As discussed earlier in this Element, weaning placed ancestral infants under 30 months of age at risk of some combination of protein energy malnutrition disease and infectious disease that could result in mortality (Bøhler & Bergström, 1995b, 1996; Bøhler et al., 1995; Fotso et al., 2013; Hailemariam & Tesfaye, 1997; Jakobsen et al., 2003; Koenig et al., 1990; Mozumder et al., 2000; Rahman et al., 1996; Ronsmans, 1996). Thus, the consequences of usurpation by a younger nursling were of such magnitude that maternal preferential attention toward a neonate, regardless of whether it involved breastfeeding, came to be interpreted as a sign of potential threat. In this way, toddlers interpreted differential treatment as a form of maternal unavailability that represented an evolutionarily relevant cue. This formulation leads to the premise that evolutionary pressures would have favored infants who responded to such cues by exhibiting strategies for managing differential treatment.

Equipped solely with separation protest, a tactic that may have once been sufficient for retaining maternal care, left infants vulnerable to sibling competition. New strategies were required. One of these involved *jealousy protest*, a presentation that is often referred to as sibling rivalry when competition or usurpation involves a sibling. In recent years, jealousy protest has been explored in laboratory research that manipulated the object of maternal attention. During an experimental condition, maternal attention is directed toward a rival in the form of a lifelike baby-doll that emits realistic cooing sounds when its abdomen is pressed. In some control conditions, maternal attention is directed toward a nonsocial object, such as a children's picture book that emits musical sounds when its pages are pressed. In others, the adult holding the baby-doll is a stranger rather than the mother.

Findings on pre-mobile infants in the 5- to 9-month age range (Draghi-Lorenz, 2010; Draghi-Lorenz et al., 2001; Hart, 2010; Hart & Carrington, 2002; Hart et al., 2004; Mize et al., 2014) revealed that in comparison with the control condition, the experimental condition elicited greater durations of crying and mother-directed approach postures for restoring both proximal and distal contact. Detailed analyses of facial affect expressions uncovered evidence of heightened durations of sadness as well as anger (see Figure 2), and inquiry into neurophysiological substrates uncovered evidence of approach-style anterior EEG activity, which is a pattern associated with the emotion of anger (He et al., 2010). Attention to infant gender revealed that the facial affect expression of fear/wariness was more prominent in females than males (see Figure 3).

Findings on mobile 9- to 28-month-olds (Fernandez et al., 2022; Hart & Behrens, 2013a; Hart et al., 1998a; Mize & Jones, 2012; Szabo et al., 2014) revealed that the experimental condition elicited increases in responses with the

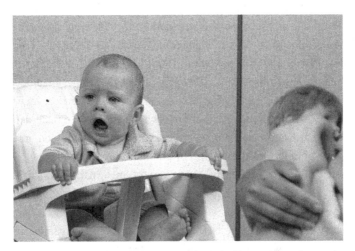

Figure 2 A 6-month-old male displays facial affect expressions of anger, fussing, and loud vocalizations as his mother directs attention to a lifelike baby-doll as if it were a real infant. Photo by Kenny Braun, courtesy of Sybil L. Hart, Texas Tech University

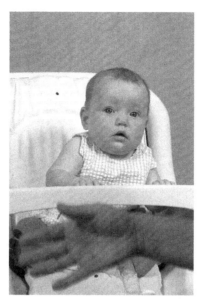

Figure 3 A 6-month-old female infant demonstrates the facial affect expression of fear/wariness and approach behavior as her mother reaches to accept a lifelike baby-doll. Photo by Kenny Braun, courtesy of Sybil L. Hart, Texas Tech University

aim of regaining unshared, proximal contact with mother (see Figure 4). These consisted of vigorous efforts to redirect maternal attention from the doll to the self by pushing the doll from the mother's lap, trying to climb onto mother's lap, and clinging. These responses were often accompanied by negatively valenced expressions of distress, such as whining, pestering, and fussing, that were interspersed with self-comforting behaviors, such as fidgeting and sucking fingers, to help attenuate distress. More acute cases involved a broad array of responses that ranged from behavioral inhibition and blunted facial affect expressions, to highly charged disinhibited expressions of alarm, including tantrums and attacks on the doll, the mother, and infants themselves.

Due to its mother-directedness, jealousy protest has been interpreted as a presentation of attachment behavior, which aligns with Bowlby's (1982) observation,

> in most young children the mere sight of mother holding another baby in her arms is enough to elicit strong attachment behaviour. The older child insists on remaining close to his mother, or on climbing on her lap. (Bowlby, 1982, p. 260)

Notably, Bowlby interpreted jealousy protest as a presentation of attachment behavior even though it is activated while a mother is present. Hence, this

Figure 4 A 10- month-old female expresses alarm and displays efforts to redirect maternal attention toward herself as her mother treats a lifelike baby-doll as if it were a real infant. Photo courtesy of Sybil L. Hart, Texas Tech University.

manner of protest is recognized as attachment behavior, not due to serving as a mechanism for attaining proximal contact with a caregiver, but rather for attaining unshared, or at least privileged, proximal contact with a caregiver (Hart, 2015, 2018, 2022a).

In addition to depicting jealousy protest as a presentation of attachment behavior, studies have unearthed evidence that point to ultimate levels of causality by uncovering results that are not easily explained simply on the basis of social experience. First, infants who had siblings, and so they were likely to have had some history of exposure to differential treatment, did not differ from infants who did not have older siblings. Also, the gender difference in the expression of fear was discovered in infants who were so young, only 6 months of age, that it could not be explained entirely on the basis of gender-specific differences in experiences of socialization. Second, replications by independent researchers from disparate regions of the United States and with ethnically diverse samples, as well as work in Europe (Szabo et al., 2014) and South America (Fernandez et al., 2022) documented comparable results. Anecdotally, similarly motivated presentations by toddlers have frequently been observed in non-Western settings (Bateson & Mead, 1942, Everett, 2014; Shostak, 1976). For example, during her appointment in Ghana, Cicely Williams (reported in Stanton, 2001) observed "uncomprehending indignation, rage and bitterness in a child of three years old who found that his place on his mother's back was suddenly usurped by a new baby" (Stanton, 2001, p. 157). These findings point to jealousy protest as species-typical behavior, which cannot be accounted for without entertaining the influence of an innate mechanism.

Furthermore, each of the studies unveiled evidence of jealousy protest outside the context of psycho-social disruption. In contrast with early accounts of jealousy as a feature of motherless refugees and toddlers being traumatized by the birth of a sibling (Freud & Dann, 1951, 1937; Levy, 1934; Winnicott, 1977, 2002) that went so far as to underpin criteria for diagnosing child psychopathology (Wolraich et al., 1996), infants in these laboratory studies were drawn from community samples absent history of changes in family structure or upheaval. This being the case, the studies illuminate a manner of responding to differential treatment that is negative in affective tone, yet it is neither atypical nor an indication of psychopathology. Certainly, we are not suggesting that experience is unimportant to jealousy protest's unfolding. Indeed, inquiry into individual differences has identified specific features of response that are statistically atypical and meaningfully associated with risk factors, including insecure quality of infant-maternal attachment, maternal depression, and maternal parenting behavior characterized by disengagement, insensitivity, and hostility (Fernandez et al., 2022; Hart, 2015; Hart et al., 1998b, 2003; Hart & Behrens, 2013a, 2013b). Thus, it appears that due to an inherited foundation, jealousy protest's unfolding occurs inevitably, yet it does so through a developmental process that operates along both normative and atypical pathways.

Finally, the validity of the laboratory paradigm is upheld by evidence that the studies generated results that cohere with descriptions of infants' responses during exposure to differential treatment in naturalistic settings, where maternal attention is directed to a real infant (Chapman & Hart, 2017). In addition, the laboratory results cohere with an ethnographic account by Margaret Mead and Gregory Bateson (Bateson & Mead, 1942) of a toddler's responses during a similar type of scenario in a naturalistic setting, located in a non-Western setting that reflected the lifestyle of hunter-gatherers. Their photographic analysis (see Figure 5, Plates 6, 7, and 8) captures a toddler-aged male infant demonstrating greater distress in Plate 8, in which his mother is shown holding his infant sister, than in Plates 6 and 7, where the mother is holding both infants. Plate 8 also illustrates what appears to be a display of jealousy protest in an instance of rivalry over access to mother's milk. In it, the younger infant is seen monopolizing both of her mother's nipples, suckling from one and clenching the other in her hand, while glaring at her brother as if attempting to ward off a competitor for mother's milk.

Figure 5 A Balinese mother with two nurslings, a toddler-aged male and younger female. In Plate 6, the mother is seated with both infants on her lap while suckling the younger infant. In Plate 7, the "mother rubs her breast to make the milk come" (Bateson & Mead, 1942, pg. 195), apparently preparing to also suckle the toddler. Plate 8 appears to illustrate rivalry over access to mother's milk. The younger sibling is held in her mother's arm while monopolizing both of her mother's nipples, suckling from one and clenching the other in her hand, while glaring down at her brother who clings to his mother's legs while reaching for her arm, as if asking to be picked up. Reprinted from *Balinese Character: A Photographic Analysis*, 1942, p. 194, with permission from the publisher, The New York Academy of Sciences

In sum, laboratory research on triadic social interaction among a mother, her infant, and rival shows that when maternal attention is directed exclusively toward the rival, it is met by her infant's presentation of attachment behavior with the goal of attaining unshared proximal contact with mother. The presentation is manifested by distress, combined with tactics for removing and replacing the rival in order to recoup preferential status, and so it is termed jealousy protest. Evidence of an inherited foundation is indicated by its commonality across culturally and ethnically diverse community samples of infants as young as 6 months that cannot be explained simply on the basis of experience.

To account for its evolved basis, we theorized that ancestral toddlers interpreted mothers' preferential treatment toward another infant as a threat-relevant cue, for it would have forecasted potential competition for mother's milk, which was an outcome that would pose mortal threat to infants under 30-months of age. Thus, evolutionary pressures favored infants who managed differential treatment by acting upon that cue through presentations of jealousy protest, and the ones with the best chances of being selected were those who were able to demonstrate it by as early as 9 months. By this age, the 9-month period of human gestation had concluded, which marked the onset of potential for the arrival of the most likely and serious rival for mother's milk, a newborn sibling. Although it is possible that the evolved basis of jealousy protest could be attributable to its adaptive value upon competition with a rival other than a younger sibling, we find it difficult to identify a competitor that would have been as compelling, whose appearance became apparent before an infant's first birthday, and was a recurrent, species-typical event that posed risk of morbidity throughout the EEA.

3.3 Weaning Distress and Parent Offspring Conflict

We have theorized that separation and jealousy protests came about due to the fitness benefits of treating maternal absence and differential treatment toward a younger infant as evolutionarily relevant cues by foreshadowing harm due to deprivation of mother's milk. It seems unlikely at these negatively valenced presentations would have been compelled, nor could they have arisen as species-typical behaviors, were it not for the probability that ancestral infants' access to mothers' milk for periods as long as 30 months was not guaranteed. As discussed earlier in the Element, the energetic and opportunity costs of lactation are substantial (Hinde & Milligan, 2011; Quinn, 2016), even for women who are not pregnant (Emmott, 2023; Salmon & Hehman, 2022; Trivers, 1974), and as Hrdy (1999) points out, mothers are not innately predisposed to make sacrifices for infants.

Given the immense costs of lactation, its 30-month duration is remarkable. Therefore, it is understandable that mothers turned to wet nurses and reliance on animal milks and soft complementary foods when these became available. However, these options were mostly unavailable prior to the Holocene (Bocquet-Appel, 2011; Dettwyler, 1995; Ellison, 1995; Howcroft et al., 2012). Until that time, the likeliest strategy for reducing the burden of lactation was to shorten its duration, and for infants under 30 months of age, this was problematic. It is also thought to have been a source of conflict between nurslings and mothers over investment allocation that is regarded as the prototypical illustration of parent–offspring conflict theory (POC; Trivers, 1974) that offspring demand more from their parents than their parents are willing to invest.

Parent–offspring conflict theory has been the basis of predictions that the mother who prohibits her infant from breastfeeding in order to retain the benefits to maternal fitness should be met by her infant's protests to prolong breastfeeding, known as *weaning distress*, in order to retain the benefits to infant fitness. Due to its fitness benefits, weaning distress is construed as an evolved psychological mechanism. However, efforts to uncover evidence of a genetic foundation have met with inconclusive results, at least in part due to the daunting task of reaching extant samples where breast milk is of importance to degrees that match levels in the EEA. In some studies (Fouts et al., 2005; Quinlan et al., 2003), data have been based on work using pastoralists where infants still had some access to sources of nutrition that could supplement breast milk. Others (Fouts & Lamb, 2005; Fouts et al., 2005) explored weaning distress among foragers through attention to children who were 36–53 months of age for whom breast milk was not imperative to survival and all of whom were consuming solid foods. Possibly, productive efforts to uncover evidence of an inherited mechanism could emerge from studies that track the process of weaning among nurslings under 30 months of age, who live in settings where there are no substitutes for mothers' milk, where health systems do not exist, and who can be observed during day and nighttime hours, and during exchanges with their mothers while breastfeeding is being denied. Ideally, these studies would also control for infants' nutritional status.

Until such evidence becomes available, we offer separation and jealousy protests. These presentations are theorized as having been compelled by stimuli that represented potential threat of deprivation of mother's milk, which is an outcome that parallels that which is associated with weaning distress. After all, deprivation of breast milk foretold morbidity and mortality, and did so regardless of whether it had been precipitated by maternal absence, maternal differential treatment, or a mother's active prohibition against breastfeeding. In addition to commonality in terms of fitness benefits, protest behaviors and weaning distress share phenotypical characteristics that pertain to their affect's valence and direction. Both separation protest (Kagan, 1976; Kagan et al., 1980; Kearsley et al., 1975; Lester et al., 1974; Super et al., 2012) and jealousy protest (Draghi-Lorenz, 2010; Draghi-Lorenz et al., 2001; Fernandez et al., 2022; Hart & Behrens, 2013a; Hart & Carrington, 2002; Hart et al., 1998a, 2004; Mize & Jones, 2012; Mize et al., 2014; Szabo et al., 2014) resemble weaning distress in that they are manifested by mother-directed fussing and crying, behaviors that were construed as indices of weaning distress in past research among foragers, and they were interpreted as such on the basis of observations of behaviors that took place outside the context of breastfeeding (Fouts et al., 2005).

Furthermore, all three presentations can be manifested by explosive anger, as in tantrums, which is behavior that is emotionally and physiologically taxing for infants (Gunnar, 2005). This being the case, it seems unlikely that protest behavior would have been presented had it not been necessitated by failure to achieve the desired results through more subtle forms of appeal. This suggests that protest behavior, like weaning distress, could have served as a "psychological weapon"

(Trivers, 1974), for engaging in conflict. Note that the behavioral repertoire of infants allows for distress to be expressed in ways that do not require confrontation. For example, when infants are disturbed by a caregiver who appears unresponsive and still-faced, they demonstrate withdrawal (Tronick et al., 1978). Similarly, when exposed to evolutionarily relevant, recurrent threats, such as snakes and dangerous plants, they recoil (Pauen & Hoehl, 2015; Wlodarczyk et al., 2018).

3.4 Conclusion

This inquiry focused on two components of the attachment behavioral system, separation protest and jealousy protest. We theorized that they came about under conditions where infants perceived maternal absence and maternal differential attention toward a younger infant as threat-relevant cues that foreshadowed potential for harm by challenging infant access to mother's milk that was imperative to survival. As cues that were recurrent, species-typical events across the EEA, they came to serve as evolutionarily relevant stimuli, and so selection pressures would have favored infants who acted upon them by deploying protest behaviors as strategies to help deter mothers from leaving or attending to a rival infant. This formulation leads to proposing that these two protest behaviors originated, not as innately based mechanisms for seeking safety that were triggered by natural cues to danger (Bowlby, 1969/1982), but rather as mechanisms for securing access to a source of breast milk. Furthermore, as the prime, if not sole, source of breast milk, an infant's own mother was the only caregiver who was imperative to infant survival, which accounts for the infant-maternal relationship arising as the only infant-caregiver relationship that is recognize as a species-wide phenomenon.

These interpretations of separation and jealousy protests also lead to theory that links the attachment behavioral system to parent–offspring conflict. If they originated, as we argue, as strategies to secure access to mothers' milk, then they would have been adaptive by addressing a goal not unlike the one associated with another mother-directed expression of negativity, weaning distress. Parallels between the two protest behaviors and weaning distress in terms of their goals in addition to commonality in terms of their affective valence and mother-directedness call attention to the possibility of yet another similarity. This one pertains to the likelihood that protest behaviors, like weaning distress, arose as tactics for engaging in conflict that were compelled by instances involving maternal resistance that led to confrontations known as parent–offspring conflict. If so, interpretations of protest behavior can be broadened so as to recognize them as attachment behaviors that were compelled not only by the need to manage threat of morbidity, but also by the need to manage maternal resistance. Judging by the attachment behavioral system's pivotal role in establishing an attachment relationship (Bowlby, 1969/1982), the idea that parent–offspring conflict played a role in its origination offers strong support for POC theory (Trivers, 1974).

4 The Affectional Nature of Attachment

By promoting contact with mother, separation and jealousy protests were foundational to attachment formation (Bowlby, 1969/1982). Yet, these are negatively valenced behaviors, and so their contribution offers little toward explaining positive emotionality that characterizes infants' bonds with mothers. In Western settings, its affective essence is captured within the title of a volume by Ainsworth (1967), "Infant Care and the Growth of Love." By referring to emotionality as "love" that "grows," she attributed it, not to an inborn mechanism, but rather to exogenous influences of caregiving. These ideas sparked attachment theorists' investigative attention to qualities of care that play a role in attachment formation which culminates in a love relationship (Ainsworth, 1964, 1967, 1969; Bowlby, 1969/1982).

Although their approaches generated a rich body of literature, the findings that emerged became difficult to interpret once cultural psychologists and anthropologists showed that caregiving practices differ across cultures, and many that are typical and adaptive in some settings appear to be irrelevant in others (Bornstein, 2002; Harkness & Super, 2002). For example, infants in most Western settings are exposed to face-to-face interaction, where they are positioned in a specially designed reclining chair directly opposite a caregiver who provides verbal stimulation in the form of "parentese" and eye contact through games, such as peek-a-boo, while nighttime hours are spent in a crib, often in a separate room. In contrast, infants in many non-Western settings can spend large portions of the day strapped to a caregiver's back, where they receive vestibular stimulation as well as physical contact that continues throughout nighttime hours of bed-sharing. In the same vein, a toddler who shows independence can be viewed in one society as bold and mature but in another as disrespectful, while a display of distress that is treated indulgently in one culture can be rejected in another (Keller & Otto, 2014; Otto & Keller, 2014).

Cultural variation has been especially problematic when it comes to the construct of attachment security (Gottlieb, 2014; Levine, 2014). Secure attachment status, that is broadly construed as an outcome of caregiving that engenders healthy parent–infant relationships, has traditionally been determined on the basis of infants' responses during eliciting conditions that involve separation from a primary caregiver and entry of strangers. These conditions were incorporated in a laboratory procedure, known as the Strange Situation Procedure (SSP, Ainsworth et al., 1978), that was originally designed to induce stress. However, evidence of cross-cultural differences in socialization practices that entail varied levels of exposure to maternal absence and strangers' presence have raised questions with respect to the validity of a procedure that is not equally stressful across cultures. Consequently, cross-cultural studies have shed light on the myriad ways in which infants are reared, yet evidence of a species-wide feature of care that could have shaped the positive valence of attachment has been elusive.

Based on this literature, it seems likely that the EEA was not a uniform environment when it came to infant care – with at least one exception. A parenting behavior that is known to have been practiced universally throughout most of evolutionary history is breastfeeding (Brines & Billeaud, 2021; Hart, 2022a; Hinde, 2014), and so we return to the topic of lactation, this time not through attention to breast *milk*, but rather to the behaviors that are responsible for its transfer to infants. Clearly, this topic is worthy of attention since breast milk offers fitness benefits that cannot be imparted without behaviors that are responsible for transferring it to infants. Even so, treatment through scientific approaches has been limited despite the fact that throughout most of prehistory breast milk has been as imperative to species survival as seminal fluid. Though it has been said that breast milk, "like semen, possessed life-giving force. While semen was necessary to create life, breast milk was necessary to sustain it" (Salmon, 1994, p. 251), in comparison with behavior that was necessary for transferring semen, less is known about behavior that was necessary for transferring breast milk.

More specifically to the aims of this Element, our attention to breastfeeding behavior responsible for milk transfer focuses on its potential contribution to the affectional nature of bonds between infants and the primary source of breast milk, infants' mothers. The possibility being entertained is far from a new idea, but one that is under-researched after it was discounted following a number of prominent reports (Darwin, 1877; Harlow, 1958) and abundant empirical evidence which made it clear that infants can form bonds of attachment with caregivers who do not breastfeed, such as fathers. However, that conclusion was based on observations that were conducted in contemporary Western settings and so they addressed proximate levels of causality, which does not preclude the possible contribution of inherited propensities and prospect that the affective component of the infant-maternal relationship could have been shaped by exogenous influences of care that were organized by breastfeeding as it featured across the wide range of ancestral settings. This leads to asking how breastfeeding worked in the EEA.

The material that follows discusses lactation-based cohesion, defined as a relationship constrained by species-typical, bio-psychosocial features of ancestral nurslings and their mothers, as well as ecological parameters of the EEA where the breastfeeding relationship is likely to have been embedded within a network of multiple caregivers. Our hope is that such an approach offers a step toward understanding how lactation-based cohesion could have anchored infants' encounters with caregivers in ways that ultimately shaped the affectional nature of attachment.

4.1 Birth to 9 Months: Exclusive Breastfeeding

In her field study of infants in Uganda, Ainsworth (1964) observed that by the age of 4–6 months, infants' smiles, vocalizations and greeting behaviors were being directed selectively toward their mothers, and by 6–7 months she noted that "following the mother became more and more consistent, as though attachment to her were becoming stronger and better consolidated. Protest at the mother's departure became more consistent too" (Ainsworth, 1964, p. 56). Her observations were later found consistent with findings of cross-cultural studies (Kagan et al., 1980; Lester et al., 1974; van IJzendoorn & Sagi, 1999), and so the 9-month-old's ability to demonstrate preferences for specific care-givers came to define a turning point in the process of attachment formation, such that it is seen as marking the onset of clear-cut attachment (Ainsworth, 1964, 1969).

Ainsworth's observation of infants' preferences for their mothers by 6–7 months is interesting in light of recent findings in the fields of infant nutrition and evolutionary biology. These indicate that for the first 6–7 months of life, ancestral infants were sustained by exclusive breastfeeding (EBF), meaning that they were fed nothing except breast milk (Dewey, 2013; Veile, 2018), and so nutritional support that they received from their mothers during this period was no less extensive than it had been during the previous 9 months *in utero*. These findings suggest an overlap between the time frame during which infants develop clear-cut attachment and the one during which ancestral infants were sustained by EBF, which may be attributable to a common origin in the EEA that can be approached by considering how EBF was experienced by ancestral infants.

First, ecological features of lactation-based cohesion included co-sleeping, which was customary to the extent that it has been interpreted as species-typical behavior (Barry, 2019, 2021; Barry & McKenna, 2022; McKenna et al., 1993; Thoman, 2006). In addition to the sheer number of hours of propinquity that it entailed, bed-sharing coincided with breastfeeding that, of course, could not occur without skin-to-skin contact, which is a salient manner of proximal contact that is known for cultivating sense of intimacy. Skin-to-skin contact has been found associated with infants presenting lower durations of crying, heightened self-regulatory skills, as well as physiological indices of superior stress regulation. These include more optimal cardio-respiratory stability, earlier capacity for thermoregulation, reduced pain during painful procedures, left frontal brain activation, improved sleep architecture, decreased stress reactivity/cortisol levels, as well as oxytocin release (Bigelow & Power, 2020; Cleveland et. al., 2017; Ionio et al., 2021; Ferroin et al., 2022; Moore et al., 2016; Northolt, 2020) that is theorized as reflecting experiences of pleasure (Hardin et al., 2020; Moberg et al., 2020, 2022). Based on these findings, it is reasonable to conclude that for ancestral infants, proximal contact via co-sleeping and skin-to-skin contact engendered psychological experiences of comfort and intimacy.

Second, EBF occurred during a time frame that occurred so early in ontogeny that it precluded competition with a newborn sibling. As discussed earlier, IBIs of less than 9 months were almost unknown, and the rare cases that occurred would have been fatal for the extant infant, if not also for the mother and neonate. Thus, EBF was experienced during a time frame when an ancestral infant was guaranteed of contact with mother that was privileged by being unshared with another nursling.

Finally, breastfeeding would have been characterized by features of lactating women that govern both the quantity and quality of caregiving. Especially during the early months, when lactogenesis is heavily dependent on frequent suckling, long intervals between feeding sessions cause milk synthesis to decline. With prolonged interruption, milk synthesis comes to a complete halt that is usually irreversible. Furthermore, stored breast milk is released by the let-down reflex that is stimulated by the infant's suckling or by external stimulation, as illustrated in Figure 5, Plate 7, by the mother who "rubs her breast to make the milk come" (Bateson & Mead, 1942, p. 195). Remarkably, it can also be stimulated simply by a mother hearing an infant cry, and in some cases, just by thinking about infant distress. In either of these cases, the let-down reflex triggers contractions that cause discomfort that is difficult to alleviate without breastfeeding. Failure to do so places mothers at risk of breast engorgement that results in medical complications, including pain and infection (Lawrence, 2022; Wambach & Spencer, 2021). It seems likely that in order to create and maintain adequate supplies of breast milk and to avoid the discomfort of the let-down reflex as well as possible health risks, ancestral mothers limited separations that were frequent or of long duration. Thus, steady exposure to proximal contact would have been experienced to a degree that is difficult to overestimate since birth weight doubles by the age of 6 months, which does not happen without substantial amounts of time devoted to feeding (Küpers et al., 2015; Woroby et al., 2009).

Importantly, lactation-based cohesion was characterized by steady contact with the breastfeeding mother that would have been inevitable regardless of whether the mother had been imbued with feelings of "mother love." Nor was it predicated on maternal beliefs about their infants' personhood. In the EEA, a "good enough mother" would have been one who, after a practical reckoning of the cost-benefit trade-offs of lactation (Salmon & Hehman, 2022), had simply decided that she wanted her infant to live. Note too that the construct of "insensitive breastfeeding" has yet to be defined, which contrasts with other sorts of feeding behaviors that can be displayed in ways that are deemed insensitive or intrusive, as indicated by treatment, such as, pressure-to-eat and food restriction (Jansen et al., 2017; van Vliet et al., 2022). Thus, from an infant's perspective, the sensitive quality of contact with mother, much like the steady quantity, can be understood as a largely built-in feature of EBF.

In sum, the first year of lactation-based cohesion was constrained by entailing EBF. This meant that ancestral infants were assured of unshared, proximal contact with one person, whose identity was predetermined, that stood out for the degree to which it imparted positively valenced psychological experiences of intimacy and privilege that were amplified by being inextricably linked with pleasurable physiological sensations associated with ingesting breast milk, satiety and enjoyment of its sweet taste. Due to the regularity of these experiences, they would have become predictable so as to have precipitated expectations of having steady and exclusive access to this nature of proximal contact with mother (Hart, 2016b, 2022b). It seems plausible that the totality of these physiological and psychological sensations would have been profoundly satisfying so that, over deep time, it gave rise to an innate mechanism that can be construed as underpinning the affectional nature of attachment.

The mechanism can also be understood as playing a role in the unfolding of clear-cut attachment by as early as 9 months, which is a remarkable achievement in social cognition. As Bowlby (1967) observed,

> When a baby is born he cannot tell one person from another and indeed can hardly tell person from thing. Yet, by his first birthday he is likely to have become a connoisseur of people. Not only does he come quickly to distinguish familiars from strangers but amongst his familiars he chooses one or more favorites. (Bowlby, 1967, p. v)

Indeed, the earliness and robustness of this phenomenon is stunning, and at least partially explained by recalling that in contrast with psychological adaptations that are attributed to recurrent, but nonuniversal, evolutionarily relevant events, such as snake bites and the arrival of a closely spaced newborn sibling that gave rise to adaptations despite having impacted only a subset of infants, exposure to EBF was universal (Hart, 2022a, 2022b).

4.2 9–30 Months: Complementary Feeding

Isotopic studies of archaeological hunter-gatherer populations and findings on extant populations of foragers suggest that complementary foods, most likely premasticated plant and animal foods, started to be provided alongside breast milk during the final quarter of the first year (Sellen & Smay, 2001; Tessone et al., 2015). This would have coincided with the juncture when breast milk alone would have been insufficient for meeting infants' nutrient needs (Dewey, 2013). Although this nature of maturation may not have been apparent to ancestral women, they would have been aware of outward signs of maturation, such as, the infant's ability to control the neck, hold the head in an upright position, and sit with support. These signs would have indicated that infants were able to consume soft foods without suckling and without choking (CDC, 2023a), which made complementary feeding possible.

The transition to complementary feeding would have set the stage for changes in the manner of care that could henceforth be provided. Because complementary foods can be fed by caregivers other than mothers, alloparents could take on greater responsibility for care, and so infants would have encountered treatment that differed from their earlier experiences within the context of EBF. The changes could have come in various ways, but contexts of cooperative childrearing would have been responsible for several that were especially likely. Some that were also especially impactful stemmed from the likelihood that increases in the quantity of allomaternal caregiving coincided with decreases in the quantity of maternal caregiving. As discussed earlier, the decrease would have violated expectations of steady exposure to exclusive proximal contact with mother, which could have provoked more frequent occasions for parent–offspring conflict. However, it would have also been responsible for exposing infants to a forum that compelled the acquisition of social skills beyond those which had been sufficient in the context of EBF.

First, it seems probable that infants' strategies for seeking care that had previously concentrated on a single, predetermined source, usually the mother, were gradually diffused among multiple caregivers. Simply dividing up bids and distributing them equally among alloparents would have been inadequate. In order to appeal to disparate caregivers whose penchants varied individually and with cultural traditions, an infant's repertoire of tactics would have become diversified as it became clear that tactics and attributes which were effective under some conditions failed in others. For example, in some cases, infants were likely to have profited from learning how to appeal to alloparents by ingratiating themselves (Hrdy & Burkart, 2022), while in others, success depended on physical attractiveness (Gottlieb, 2014). Still other settings called for the ability to identify opportune sources of care. This would require the ability to discern which caregivers were better sources of stimulation and play, which were inclined to be responsive in times of hunger or distress, and how to navigate social settings marked by conflict among the caregivers themselves (Meehan & Hawks, 2014). Numerous accounts of infants being passed among an unpredictable assortment of caregivers, depending on who happened to be present and willing at any given time, would have called for a degree of sociality that is outstanding and unique to humans (Buttelman, 2022; Locke & Bogin, 2022).

Social adeptness that promoted the ancestral infant's ability to acquire care would have been especially adaptive for those whose mothers had become pregnant or had already given birth. It has been suggested that the early introduction of complementary feeding and its extended duration may have coevolved with humans' unique cooperative childrearing system so that allomaternal caregivers could take on greater responsibility for the care of infants (Emmott & Page, 2019; Martin, 2017), and the advantages to toddler-aged weanlings would have been especially significant. As discussed earlier, a closely spaced subsequent pregnancy or childbirth would have compelled early weaning of existing toddlers while they still depended on mothers' milk for nutrition and passive resistance to disease. Nevertheless, some did not succumb to morbidity, while some of the older ones may have even thrived. It seems unlikely that these weanlings could have done so without the support of allomaternal caregivers who could provide sustenance.

Finally, unlike care during the first year that was mostly unshared, toddlers would have found themselves in settings that were competitive since it was likely that other infants were present and in need of care from the very same pool of potential caregivers. This scenario could have added impetus to infants' efforts to expand and perfect their repertoire of tactics for soliciting care. They would also learn from observing maternal exertions to scaffold and otherwise improve chances of securing allomaternal support, as well as the consequences of failure. For example, Gottlieb (2014) described how a West African Beng mother who, in order to be able to go to work, felt compelled to subject her infant to an hour-long regimen of grooming so as to entice the support of allomaternal caregivers who were enthralled by another especially attractive child. One of the lessons learned was that nonmaternal caregivers could refuse to provide care, in which case the burden of childcare belonged to mothers.

Another possible outcome pertains to sentiment that corresponds with an infant feeling unwanted by alloparents, but not by mothers, due to being insufficiently cute.

4.3 30–36 Months: Weaning

Complementary feeding is thought to have continued until ancestral infants approached the third birthday, at which point breastfeeding was brought to conclusion (Clayton et al., 2006; Eerkens & Bartelink, 2013; Loponte & Mazza, 2021; Tessone et al, 2015; Veile & Miller, 2021; Waters-Rist et al., 2011). Given the magnitude of the costs involved in lactation, the fact that it lasted for a minimum of three years reflects a level of investment that is remarkable, and not easily explained. It seems unlikely that the extended duration of lactation could have been based on mothers understanding that until infants' digestive and immune systems had matured, at the age of 30 months, breast milk was necessary for providing passive resistance to disease. Nor could mothers have been motivated by appreciating lactation for its role in regulating fecundity by interfering with the release of hormones necessary for triggering ovulation so that IBIs could last as long as 4 years, which helped prevent morbidity, not only in infants but also in mothers themselves (Razzaque et al., 2005; Shachar & Lyell, 2012). However, they would have recognized the appearance of full dentition, and they would have appreciated molar teeth for their importance to chewing tough meat, roots, and nuts without having to be premasticated. This meant that infants' metabolic requirements could be satisfied without breast milk, and weaning could be brought to conclusion (Dettwyler, 1995; Hart, 2022a, 2022b; Humphrey, 2010; Locke & Bogin, 2022; Smith, 2013).

Physiological maturation that governed the infant's capacity for food intake would again have implications for the nature of infant–caregiver social dynamics. Weaning coincided, not only with the eruption of full dentition and maturation of the infant's digestive and immune systems, but also with the point when the infant–caregiver attachment relationship is theorized as reaching consolidation. Thus, weaning would have taken place following a 2-year period of complementary feeding that had provided them, not only with a platform for developing confidence in maternal availability (Ainsworth, 1969, 1972; Bowlby, 1969/1982, 1973, 1980; Feeny & Woodhouse, 2016; Mikulincer & Shaver, 2019), but also with opportunities to acquire at least some of the relationships and deftness that were necessary for functioning in complex social environments where levels of maternal support were seriously reduced. At this juncture, it was no longer the case that lactation-based cohesion was imperative to infant survival. Thus, the infant-maternal relationship could transition from one that was anchored by physiological imperatives to one that rested on a psychological mechanism, fully formed attachment, untethered to lactation. Possibly, the timing of the eruption of molar teeth and maturation of infants' digestive and immune systems coevolved so as to have played a role in preventing parenting behavior as costly as breastfeeding from concluding until lactation-based cohesion had ensured that necessary social skills and supports were in place (Hart, 2022a).

Even so, it is notable that although the infant-maternal relationship is thought to be consolidated by the time ancestral infants were fully weaned, it is not rare for especially acute instances of protest behaviors to be demonstrated at this juncture. Often referred to as weaning distress since they coincide with weaning, these protests can coincide with other stressors, usually usurpation (Ainsworth, 1967; Bateson & Mead, 1942; Shostak, 1976). For example, in an ethnographic report on the Pirahã, a hunter-gatherer society living in the Amazon rainforest in Brazil, Daniel Everett (2014) attributed a child's presentation of protest behavior not only to deprivation of mother's milk, but also to losses of both intimacy and privileged status,

> During the day, one sees children throwing tantrums as a protest against being hungry, cut off from mother's milk, and losing the privilege of its mother's arms to a newborn infant. I have seen young children writhing in the dirt screaming, pounding their faces with their fists, deliberately throwing themselves full force on the ground, not infrequently close to or even in the fire (serious burns have occurred), spitting, and carrying on as though they were in the throes of epilepsy. (Everett, 2014, pp.180)

Although acute disturbances of this nature could be aberrations that reflect atypical psychosocial development, Everett described them as typical of Pirahã children, who, following an adjustment period that lasted several weeks, showed no sign of maladjustment. The outbursts are also perplexing given that they have been observed in toddlers who were being reared in societies where cooperative childrearing was normative, and where it seems likely that some of children's relationships with alloparents would have been consistent with attachment (Meehan & Hawks, 2014). Perhaps, despite the availability of supportive alloparents, these disturbances result from some combination of hunger and expectations of intimacy and privileged status that are specific to mothers, and do not apply to other caregivers, even those who may be attachment figures. Indeed, literature on cooperative child rearing rarely mentions similarly acute presentations being directed at nonmaternal caregivers. This leads to speculation that there may be more than one type of infant–caregiver attachment relationship, and the bond which connects infants to mothers may not be identical to the one that connects them to other attachment figures.

4.4 Final Conclusion

In earlier sections of this Element, separation and jealousy protests were interpreted as attachment behaviors that came about as adaptations to mortal threat (Bowlby, 1969/1982) of morbidity. As such, these protest behaviors were construed as having been compelled by conditions where maternal absence and differential treatment toward a younger infant presaged impaired access to mother's milk that was imperative to infant health. We theorized that by helping secure mothers' close and undivided attention, these protests were adaptive toward managing access to mothers' milk. In addition, these protest behaviors were theorized as having been compelled by maternal resistance, and so they were necessary for managing confrontations with mother that resulted in parent–offspring conflict. We also proposed that the prominence of the infant-maternal relationship arose from ancestral conditions where mothers were the only caregivers who were essential to survival due to being irreplaceable since, in most cases, they were the only dedicated sources of breast milk without which infants could not survive.

In this section, we turned to exploring positive affect that characterizes the attachment relationship, and our interest in its evolved basis called for inquiry into a context of care that was a species-typical feature of the EEA. This led to addressing care that involved breastfeeding and how it would have been organized by features of infants' physiological maturation that governed food intake. We reasoned that the first year was limited by infants' sole reliance on breast milk, which mandated EBF. The second and third years were enabled by the infant's ability to hold the neck and head upright and sit with support, which made complementary feeding possible. By 30 months, maturation of the immune and digestive systems released infants from reliance on breast milk, while the eruption of full dentition meant that solid foods could be consumed without being premasticated, which made it possible for breastfeeding to be brought to conclusion. This progression in the infant's capacity for food intake would have orchestrated distinct platforms for social interactions, each responsible for precipitating distinct kinds of experiences, expectations, and psychological adaptations that could have played a role in shaping the propensity to form different kinds of attachment relationships.

During the first 7 to 9 months, when infants were sustained by EBF, social experiences would have centered on one person whose identity was predetermined, usually the mother, who would have been a steady source of satiety and psychological sensations of intimacy and privilege that was profoundly satisfying. We theorized that by occurring predictably, uniformly, and universally across the EEA over deep time, this manner of contact gave rise to an adaptation that underpins the affectional nature of attachment to mothers by engendering positive affect that can be described as love that is imbued with sense of belonging and entitlement.

For the next 2 years of complementary feeding, when breast milk was not the sole source of sustenance, separation from mother became more frequent and extensive, at least during daytime hours. At the time of Bowlby's writing, separation from a primary caregiver was atypical and regarded as a source of maladaptation. However, in the context of cooperative child rearing, that was a species-typical feature of the EEA, separation from mother was not only typical, but also adaptive. In comparison with the more circumscribed and uniform number and types of experiences that infants had encountered during the first year, the next 24 months involved increasing exposure to social contexts that were complex, competitive, and unpredictable. Therefore, it seems plausible that evolutionary pressures would have favored infants who were able to thrive in such challenging environments due to having been endowed with psychological plasticity and aptitude for sociality that is flexible and keen (Bjorklund, 2022). Possibly, this attribute also shaped the infant's propensity to form different kinds of attachment relationships, so that the bonds formed with nonmaternal caregivers differed from the one with mothers.

By the ancestral infant's third birthday, when weaning could come to conclusion, it was no longer the case that infant survival depended on breast milk. According to attachment theorists, this point in time also corresponds with potential for a transition whereby the infant–caregiver attachment relationship could become a fully formed, goal-corrected partnership, having been consolidated on the basis of experiences that had generated confidence in the primary caregiver as a stable source of support (Ainsworth, 1969; Ainsworth et al., 1972, 1978; Waters et al., 1991). Alternatively, it is possible that weaning coincided with the point when ancestral infants had developed confidence, not in their mothers, but in themselves. Ideally, as toddlers ventured from the cradle of EBF, their growing sense of autonomy and agency that stimulated exploration (Baillargeon et al., 2011; Bowlby, 1969/1982; Hart, 2022b) was enhanced by exposure to a rich social milieu that offered opportunities to select "favorite" (Bowlby, 1967) alloparental caregivers.

Thus, the 36-month-long period of attachment formation included a relatively lengthy period of complementary feeding during which contact with alloparents gradually increased, thereby serving as a bridge that scaffolded infant readiness for transferring dependence from mothers to nonmaternal caregivers. At the same time, it seems possible that the affectional component of attachment to mothers could have reached consolidation at a point considerably earlier than 36 months. Perhaps it was fully formed by the point during the second year when separation protest peaks (Kagan, 1976; Kagan et al., 1980; Kearsley et al., 1975), or even by as early as 9 months, when clear-cut attachment is evident. In either case, from that point onward, maternal caregiving can be understood as a mechanism, not so much for consolidating a bond, as for letting go of one.

5 Applications

We have proposed that the adaptive value of exclusivity in the infant-maternal relationship in conjunction with expectations of privileged access to mothers that arose in the context of EBF contributed to the evolved basis of jealousy protest. Insight into the origin of this instance of protest behavior may be helpful toward understanding and managing adjustment problems in toddlers upon the birth of a sibling which is an event that challenges privileged status in the child–caregiver relationship even in contemporary settings (Wolraich et al., 1996).

Disturbances at this juncture have been indicated by a wide range of internalizing and externalizing behaviors that differ with child characteristics, such as temperamental irritability and attachment security, as well as family dynamics, such as, marital and co-parental relationship functioning, parenting strategies, and disciplinary tactics, as well as parent characteristics, such as sense of efficacy, anxiety and depression. They have also often been considered in relation to ecological conditions that can coincide with a sibling's birth, such as deterioration in the quality of maternal caregiving that eventuates from childbirth and the demands of caring for a newborn infant (Chen et al., 2022; Taylor & Kogan, 1973; Teti et al., 1996; Volling et al., 2017). Essentially, this is a body of literature where there is implicit, and sometimes explicit, recognition that jealousy is involved in child disturbances that appear at this juncture. Yet, jealousy has rarely been addressed, and only indirectly, usually through questionnaires that probe the quality of the child-newborn infant sibling relationship, and while some items might pertain to usurpation, others clearly do not.

Moreover, such treatment has been limited to recognizing jealousy's contribution strictly as an outcome variable. However, it is now apparent that jealousy protest is within the infant's repertoire well before it is presented upon a newborn sibling's arrival. This raises the possibility that jealousy protest can operate, not only as an outcome variable, but also as a predictor of child adjustment at this juncture. Insight into jealousy protest as a predictor variable has emerged from evidence that when expectant mothers were given the opportunity to observe their toddlers' responses during a simple laboratory procedure that simulates the arrival of a newborn sibling, mothers found the procedure to have been a valid predictor of their child's adjustment when the new baby arrived (Chapman & Hart, 2017). This was an expected result since presentations of jealousy protest covary with the quality of infant–caregiver attachment (Fernandez et al., 2022; Hart & Behrens, 2013a; Murphy et al., 2020), which is a child characteristic that predicts levels of child adjustment following a sibling's birth (Teti & Abelard, 1989; Touris et al., 1995; Volling et al., 2023).

The procedure also had practical applications that may be of use to clinicians. By being provided with a preview of their toddler's troubled response to usurpation, mothers appreciated the procedure for illuminating the importance of taking time to help their toddlers prepare for the upcoming transition by offering support and promoting skills in emotion regulation. In addition, mothers of toddlers whose presentations were especially acute felt that the experience helped them formulate realistic expectations of their toddlers, which helped avert the possibility of feeling disappointed in their toddlers and in themselves when the new baby arrived. Even in a community sample and in the absence of established risk factors, toddlers' responses during this procedure differ widely, and acute disturbances are not rare since usurpation can be a painful experience, even for well-adjusted and otherwise mild-tempered infants of loving parents.

In conclusion, the half century since the publication of Bowlby's seminal work (1969/1982) has been one during which much has been learned about the EEA and lactation. Bowlby conceptualized the attachment behavioral system as comprised of separate classes of behaviors. These included *oral behavior*, specifically sucking, that was independent of *non-oral behaviors*, as in clinging and following, that elicit social support and stimulation. This dichotomy coheres with current understanding that the benefits of breast milk to infant health are not the same as the benefits of proximal contact with a sensitive caregiver to psychological adjustment. Although there are data which suggest that milk production involves hormonal and neurological mechanisms that may help support mothers' propensities to bond with their infants (Hart, 2022a), there is little evidence that milk consumption, for all its benefits to infant health and wellbeing, relates to infants' propensities to bond with their mothers.

However, it was Bowlby's understanding that feeding and nonfeeding behaviors start off as separate classes of behaviors, but "in the normal course of development they become integrated" (Bowlby, 1958, p. 40). In fact, the eventual integration of these distinct classes of infant behaviors would have been inevitable "in the normal course of development" within the context of lactation-based cohesion, when all infants were breastfed by their mothers and so the benefits of breast milk were inseparable from those of sensitive caregiving. However, it is no longer inevitable that feeding and nonfeeding behaviors eventually become fused with each other. In Western industrialized settings, 3 years of breastfeeding is not normative (Emmott, 2023). Formula is readily available, wet-nursing is less popular than it was prior to the advent of formula but is still an option, and, increasingly, milk banks provide access to pasteurized donor human milk. In cases where suckling is not feasible, nutrition is deliverable through medical interventions that involve tube feeding. Furthermore, soft complementary foods are widely available, as are functional health systems that further reduce infant reliance on mother's milk for resistance to disease.

Nevertheless, modern methods and conditions of feeding that enable diminished reliance on breast milk have not been without implications for infant–caregiver attachment. Clearly, the infant's diminished reliance on breast milk is not matched by diminished reliance on appropriate social stimulation and supportive relationships with sensitive caregivers (Bakermans-Kranenburg, 2021; Beebe et al., 2010), which is a problem since there is no mechanism by which sensitive care is guaranteed to the extent that was typical in the context of lactation-based cohesion. Unfortunately, the absence of such guarantees has been a factor in cases of impaired psycho-social development in young children. It has also become apparent that nonfeeding behaviors may be as crucial to infant survival as feeding behaviors (Cicchetti et al., 2006; Luby et al., 2009). Tragically, this became evident when, despite being given basic care, institutionalized infants were found unable to develop physically and mentally, and in some cases die, due to having been denied normal levels of appropriate social stimulation (Fox et al., 2013; Mackes et al., 2020; Souag-Barke et al., 2017; Spitz, 1945).

We have argued for recognizing infant-maternal attachment formation as an outgrowth of contact that was, not only profoundly satisfying, but also guaranteed by the ancestral infant's experience of EBF during the first year and continued reliance on breastmilk for the next 2 years in settings where there were no substitutes for breast milk and the only mechanism for its transfer to infants was by breastfeeding. Thus, it is a framework that offers an evolved basis for conceptualizing attachment formation as a 36-month-long process. Our hope is that it lends weight to arguments by parents, educators, and policymakers that despite any number of ways in which human behavior has been modified by modern-day methods of milk transfer, healthy psycho-social development still requires years of investment in appropriate caregiving. In many cases, it requires investment that is more costly than parents can provide without sufficient support, and so, we add to calls for policies and interventions that offer high quality, consistent support for programs, such as family leave and high-quality childcare, that extend through the first 36 months of life.

Abbreviations

Environment of evolutionary adaptedness (EEA). The physical and social environments in which humans evolved. The EEA is not a single environment, but rather the amalgamation of all the times and places under which humans faced evolutionary pressures.

Inter-birth interval (IBI). The time, usually reported as number of months, between two successive births. Normally, the duration is nine months longer than the IPI.

Inter-pregnancy interval (IPI). The time, usually reported as number of months, between the end of one pregnancy and the beginning of another. Normally it is nine months less than the IBI.

Parent–offspring conflict (POC). Disagreement between parents and offspring over the degree to which parents should invest resources in offspring. Theory holds that conflict arises since offspring demand more of parents than parents are willing to invest.

Protein energy malnutrition (PEM). A range of conditions that arise from lack of dietary protein and/or energy (calories). The condition usually affects children and is associated with co-morbidities that increase the likelihood of death.

Under-five mortality rate (U5MR). The estimated number of deaths among children under 60 months of age, usually reported as a ratio per 1,000 live births.

Exclusive breastfeeding (EBF). A manner of breastfeeding that the World Health Organization (WHO) defines as providing infants with breast milk, and no other liquids or solids, not even water, with the exception of oral rehydration solution, or drops/syrups of vitamins, minerals or medicines.

References

Ainsworth, M. D. (1964). Patterns of attachment behavior shown by the infant in interaction with his mother. *Merrill-Palmer Quarterly of Behavior and Development*, **10(1)**, 51–58. www.jstor.org/stable/23082925.

Ainsworth, M. (1967). *Infancy in Uganda: Infant Care and the Growth of Love*. Johns Hopkins University Press.

Ainsworth, M. D. S. (1969). Object relations, dependency, and attachment: A theoretical review of the infant-mother relationship. *Child Development*, **40**, 969–1025. https://doi.org/10.2307/1127008.

Ainsworth, M. D. S., Bell, S. M., & Stayton, D. J. (1972). Individual differences in the development of some attachment behaviors. *Merrill-Palmer Quarterly of Behavior and Development*, **18(2)**, 123–143. www.jstor.org/stable/23083966.

Ainsworth, M. D. S., Blehar, M. C., Waters, E., & Wall, S. (1978). *Patterns of Attachment: A Psychological Study of the Strange Situation*. Erlbaum.

Alberda, C., Graf, A., & McCargar, L. (2006). Malnutrition: Etiology, consequences, and assessment of a patient at risk. *Best Practice & Research Clinical Gastroenterology*, **20(3)**, 419–439. http://dx.doi.org/10.1016/j.bpg.2006.01.006.

Alderman, H., & Fernald, L. (2017). The nexus between nutrition and early childhood development. *Annual Review of Nutrition*, **37**, 447–476. http://dx.doi.org/10.1146/annurev-nutr-071816-064627.

American Pregnancy Association (2023). Breastfeeding during Pregnancy. https://americanpregnancy.org/ (Accessed January 1, 2023).

Andegiorgish, A. K., Woldu, H. G., Elhoumed, M., Zhu, Z., & Zeng, L. (2022). Trends of under-five mortality and associated risk factors in Zambia: A multi survey analysis between 2007 and 2018. *BMC Pediatrics*, **22(1)**, 1–12. http://dx.doi.org/10.1186/s12887-022-03362-7.

Armitage, S. J., Jasim, S. A., Marks, A. E. et al. (2011). The southern route "out of Africa": Evidence for an early expansion of modern humans into Arabia. *Science*, **331(6016)**, 453–456. http://10.1126/science.1199113.

Bahwal, S. A., Jawass, M. A., & Naji, F. S. (2020). Risk factors, comorbidities and outcomes of severe acute malnutrition among children in Mukalla Maternity and Child Hospital, Hadhramout, Yemen. *Hadhramout University Journal of Natural & Applied Sciences*, **17**, 1–9. https://digitalcommons.aaru.edu.jo/huj_nas/vol17/iss1/1.

Bakermans-Kranenburg, M. J. (2021). The limits of the attachment network. *New Directions for Child and Adolescent Development*, **2021(180)**, 117–124. http://10.1002/cad.20432.

Ballard, O., & Morrow, A. L. (2013). Human milk composition: Nutrients and bioactive factors. *Pediatric Clinics*, **60(1)**, 49–74. https://doi.org/ 10.1016/j.pcl.2012.10.002.

Barr, R. G., Konner, M., Bakeman, R., & Adamson, L. (1991). Crying in !Kung San infants: A test of the cultural specificity hypothesis. *Developmental Medicine & Child Neurology*, **33(7)**, 601–610. https://doi.org/10.1111/ j.1469-8749.1991.tb14930.x.

Barrett, H. C. (2015). Adaptations to predators and prey. In D. M. Buss, ed., *The Handbook of Evolutionary Psychology*. Wiley, pp. 200–224. https://doi.org/ 10.1002/9780470939376.ch7.

Barry, E. S. (2019). Co-sleeping as a proximal context for infant development: The importance of physical touch. *Infant Behavior and Development*, **57**, 101385. https://doi.org/10.1016/j.infbeh.2019.101385.

Barry, E. S. (2021). Sleep consolidation, sleep problems, and co-sleeping: Rethinking normal infant sleep as species-typical. *The Journal of Genetic Psychology*, **182(4)**, 183–204. https://doi.org/10.1080/00221325.2021.1905599.

Barry, E. S., & McKenna, J. J. (2022). Reasons mothers bedshare: A review of its effects on infant behavior and development. *Infant Behavior and Development*, **66**, 101684. https://doi.org/10.1016/j.infbeh.2021.101684.

Bateson, G., & Mead, M. (1942). *Balinese Character: A Photographic Analysis*. The New York Academy of Sciences.

Batool, R., Butt, M. S., Sultan, M. T., Saeed, F., & Naz, R. (2015). Protein–energy malnutrition: A risk factor for various ailments. *Critical Reviews in Food Science and Nutrition*, **55(2)**, 242–253. https://doi.org/10.1080/ 10408398.2011.651543.

Baildam, E. M., Wilier, V. F., Ward, B. S. et al. (1995). Duration and pattern of crying in the first year of life. *Developmental Medicine & Child Neurology*, **37(4)**, 345–353. https://doi.org/10.1111/j.1469-8749.1995.tb12012.x.

Baillargeon, R. H., Sward, G. D., Keenan, K., & Cao, G. (2011). Opposition-defiance in the second year of life: A population-based cohort study. *Infancy*, **16(4)**, 418–434. https://doi.org/10.1111/j.1532-7078.2010.00043.x.

Bauserman, M., Nowak, K., Nolen, T. L. et al. (2020). The relationship between birth intervals and adverse maternal and neonatal outcomes in six low and lower-middle income countries. *Reproductive Health*, **17(2)**, 1–10. https:// doi.org/10.1186/s12978-020-01008-4.

Beebe, B., Jaffe, J., Markese, S. et al. (2010). The origins of 12-month attachment: A microanalysis of 4-month mother–infant interaction. *Attachment & Human Development*, **12(1–2)**, 3–141. https://doi.org/10.1080/14616730903338985.

Bekele, H., Jima, G. H., & Regesu, A. H. (2020). Undernutrition and associated factors among lactating women: Community-based cross-sectional study in

Moyale District, Borena Zone, Southern Ethiopia. *Advances in Public Health*, 2020, **4367145**, 1–10. https://doi.org/10.1155/2020/4367145.

Benjamin, O., & Lappin, S. L. (2021). Kwashiorkor. www.ncbi.nlm.nih.gov/books/NBK507876 (Accessed December 9, 2022).

Beyer, R. M., Krapp, M., Eriksson, A., & Manica, A. (2021). Climatic windows for human migration out of Africa in the past 300,000 years. *Nature Communications*, **12(1)**, 1–10. https://doi.org/10.17605/OSF.IO/NMS4F.

Bhutta, Z. A., Berkley, J. A., Bandsma, R. H. et al. (2017). Severe childhood malnutrition. *Nature Reviews Disease Primers*, **3(1)**, 1–18. https://doi.org/10.1038/nrdp.2017.67.

Bigelow, A. E., & Power, M. (2020). Mother–infant skin-to-skin contact: Short-and long-term effects for mothers and their children born full-term. *Frontiers in Psychology*, **11, 1921**. https://doi.org/10.3389/fpsyg.2020.01921.

Bjorklund, D. F. (2015). Developing adaptations. *Developmental Review*, **38**, 13–35. https://doi.org/10.1016/j.dr.2015.07.002.

Bjorklund, D. F. & Hart, S. L. (2022). Infancy through the lens of evolutionary developmental science. In S. L. Hart & D. F. Bjorklund, eds., *Evolutionary Perspectives on Infancy*. Springer, pp. 3–15. https://doi.org/10.1007/978-3-030-76000-7_1.

Bjorklund, D. F. & Blasi, C. H. (2015). Evolutionary developmental psychology. In D. M. Buss, ed., *The Handbook of Evolutionary Psychology*. Wiley, pp. 828–850. https://doi.org/10.1002/9780470939376.ch29.

Bjorklund, D. F. (2022). Human evolution and the neotenous infant. In S. L. Hart & D. F. Bjorklund, eds., *Evolutionary Perspectives on Infancy*. Springer, pp. 19–38. https://doi.org/10.1007/978-3-030-76000-7_2.

Black, R. E., Morris, S. S., & Bryce, J. (2003). Where and why are 10 million children dying every year? *The Lancet*, **361(9376)**, 2226–2234. https://doi.org/10.1016/S0140-6736(03)13779-8.

Black, M. M., Pérez-Escamilla, R., & Rao, S. F. (2015). Integrating nutrition and child development interventions: Scientific basis, evidence of impact, and implementation considerations. *Advances in Nutrition*, **6(6)**, 852–859. https://doi.org/10.3945/an.115.010348.

Bocquet-Appel, J. P. (2011). When the world's population took off: The springboard of the Neolithic demographic transition. *Science*, **333(6042)**, 560–561. https://doi.org/10.1126/science.1208880.

Bogin, B. (2011). !Kung nutritional status and the original "affluent society" – A new analysis. *Anthropologischer Anzeiger*, **68(4)**, 349–366. www.jstor.org/stable/41262771.

Bøhler E., & Bergström S. (1995a). Premature weaning in East Bhutan: Only if mother is pregnant again. *Journal of Biosocial Science*, **27(3)**, 253–265. https://doi.org/10.1017/S0021932000022781.

Bøhler, E., & Bergström, S. (1995b). Subsequent pregnancy affects morbidity of previous child. *Journal of Biosocial Science*, **27(4)**, 431–442. https://doi.org/10.1017/S002193200002304X.

Bøhler E., & Bergström S. (1996). Child growth during weaning depends on whether mother is pregnant again. *Journal of Tropical Pediatrics*, **42**, 104–109. https://doi.org/10.1093/tropej/42.2.104.

Bøhler E., Singey J., & Bergstrom S. (1995). Subsequent pregnancy affects nutritional status of previous child: A study from Bhutan. *Acta Paediatrica*, **84**, 478–483. https://doi.org/10.1111/j.1651-2227.1995.tb13678.x.

Boldsen, J. L., Milner, G. R., & Ousley, S. D. (2022). Paleodemography: From archaeology and skeletal age estimation to life in the past. *American Journal of Biological Anthropology*, **178**, 115–150. https://doi.org/10.1111/j.1651-2227.1995.tb13678.x.

Bornstein, M. H. (2002). Parenting infants. In M. H. Bornstein, ed., *Handbook of Parenting*. Erlbaum, pp. 3–43.

Bowlby, J. (1953). Some pathological processes set in train by early mother-child separation. *Journal of Mental Science*, **99(415)**, 265–272. http://doi.org/10.1192/bjp.99.415.265.

Bowlby, J. (1958). The nature of the child's tie to his mother. *International Journal of Psychoanalysis*, **39**, 350–373.

Bowlby, J. (1967). Foreword. In M. S. Ainsworth, ed., *Infancy in Ugandasa: Infant Care and the Growth of Love*. Johns Hopkins University Press, pp. v – vi.

Bowlby, J. (1969/82). *Attachment and Loss, Vol 1, Attachment*. Basic Books.

Bowlby, J. (1973). *Attachment and Loss, Vol. 2, Separation: Anxiety and Anger*. Basic Books.

Bowlby, J. (1980). *Attachment and Loss, Vol. 3, Loss: Sadness and Depression*. Basic Books.

Bowlby, J. (1982). Attachment and loss: Retrospect and prospect. *American Journal of Orthopsychiatry*, **52(4)**, 664–678. https://doi.org/10.1111/j.1939-0025.1982.tb01456.x.

Bowlby, J., Robertson, J., & Rosenbluth, D. (1952). A two-year-old goes to hospital. *The Psychoanalytic Study of the Child*, **7(1)**, 82–94. https://doi.org/10.1080/00797308.1952.11823154.

Briend, A., Wojtyniak, B., & Rowland, M. G. (1988). Breast feeding, nutritional state, and child survival in rural Bangladesh. *British Medical Journal*

(Clinical Research Edition), **296(6626)**, 879–882. https://doi.org/10.1136/bmj.296.6626.879.

Brines, J., & Billeaud, C. (2021). Breast-feeding from an evolutionary perspective. *Healthcare*, **9**, 1–11. 10.3390/healthcare9111458. https://doi.org/10.3390/healthcare9111458.

Bryant, C. A. (2006). Nursing the adopted infant. *The Journal of the American Board of Family Medicine*, **19(4)**, 374–379. https://doi.org/10.3122/jabfm.19.4.374.

Buikstra, J. E., & Konigsberg, L. W. (1985). Paleodemography: Critiques and controversies. *American Anthropologist*, **87(2)**, 316–333. https://doi.org/10.1525/aa.1985.87.2.02a00050.

Burke, A., Kageyama, M., Latombe, G. et al. (2017). Risky business: The impact of climate and climate variability on human population dynamics in Western Europe during the Last Glacial Maximum. *Quaternary Science Reviews*, **164**, 217–229. https://doi.org/10.1016/j.quascirev.2017.04.001.

Buttelman, D. (2022). What is unique in infant thinking about others? Infant social cognition from an evolutionary perspective. In S. L. Hart & D. F. Bjorklund, eds., *Evolutionary Perspectives on Infancy*. Springer, pp. 277–302. https://doi.org/10.1007/978-3-030-76000-7_13.

Centers for Disease Control and Prevention (CDC, 2023a). When, What, and How to Introduce Solid Foods. www.cdc.gov/nutrition/infantandtoddlernutrition/foods-and-drinks/when-to-introduce-solid-foods.html (Accessed March 19, 2023).

Centers for Disease Control and Prevention (CDC, 2023b). How Long Should a Mother Breastfeed? www.cdc.gov/breastfeeding/faq/index.htm#howlong (Accessed February 17, 2023).

Chapman, J. K., & Hart, S. L. (2017). The transition from mother-of-one to mother-of-two: Mothers' perceptions of themselves and their relationships with their firstborn children. *Infant Mental Health Journal*, **38(4)**, 475–485. https://doi.org/10.1002/imhj.21650.

Chen, B. B., Ning, M., & Lv, J. (2022). Developmental trajectories of children's sibling jealousy after the birth of a sibling: Strict parental control, parenting stress and parental depression as pre-birth predictors. *Journal of Social and Personal Relationships*, **40(5)**, 1601–1621. https://doi.org/10.1177/0265407522113107.

Chikhungu, L. C., Newell, M. L., & Rollins, N. (2017). Under-five mortality according to maternal survival: A systematic review and meta-analysis. *Bulletin of the World Health Organization*, **95(4)**, 281. http://doi.org/10.2471/BLT.15.157149.

Christian, P. (2008). Infant mortality. In R. D. Semba & M. W. Bloem (eds.), *Nutrition and Health in Developing Countries*, 2nd ed. Humana, pp. 87–111. https://doi.org/10.1007/978-1-59745-464-3_4.

Cicchetti, D., Rogosch, F. A., & Toth, S. L. (2006). Fostering secure attachment in infants in maltreating families through preventive interventions. *Development and Psychopathology*, **18(3)**, 623–649. https://doi.org/10.1017/S0954579406060329.

Clavano, N. R. (1982). Mode of feeding and its effect on infant mortality and morbidity. *Journal of Tropical Pediatrics*, **28(6)**, 287–293. https://doi.org/10.1093/tropej/28.6.287.

Clayton, F., Sealy, J., & Pfeiffer, S. (2006). Weaning age among foragers at Matjes River Rock Shelter, South Africa, from stable nitrogen and carbon isotope analyses. *American Journal of Physical Anthropology: The Official Publication of the American Association of Physical Anthropologists*, **129** (2), 311–317. https://doi.org/10.1002/ajpa.20248.

Cleveland, L., Hill, C. M., Pulse, W. S. et al. (2017). Systematic review of skin-to-skin care for full-term, healthy newborns. *Journal of Obstetric, Gynecologic & Neonatal Nursing*, **46(6)**, 857–869. https://doi.org/10.1016/j.jogn.2017.08.005.

Crittenden, A. N., & Schnorr, S. L. (2017). Current views on hunter-gatherer nutrition and the evolution of the human diet. *American Journal of Physical Anthropology*, **162**, 84–109. https://doi.org/10.1002/ajpa.23148.

Dadi, A. F. (2015). A systematic review and meta-analysis of the effect of short birth interval on infant mortality in Ethiopia. *PloS one*, **10(5)**, e0126759. **C.** https://doi.org/10.1371/journal.pone.0126759.

Darwin, C. (1877). Biographical sketch of an infant. *Mind*, **2**, 285–294. www.jstor.org/stable/2246907.

Dawkins, R. (1976). *The Selfish Gene*. Oxford University Press.

de Onis, M. (2008). Child growth and development. In R. D. Semba & M. W. Bloem, eds., *Nutrition and Child Health in Developing Countries*, 2nd ed. Humana, pp. 113–138. https://doi.org/10.1007/978-1-59745-464-3_3.

De Souza, R. G. (2006). Body size and growth: The significance of chronic malnutrition among the Casiguran Agta. *Annals of Human Biology*, **33(5–6)**, 604–619. https://doi.org/10.1080/03014460601062759.

DeSilva, J. M. (2022). Childbirth and infant care in early human ancestors: What the bones tell us. In S. L. Hart & D. F. Bjorklund, eds., *Evolutionary Perspectives on Infancy*. Springer, pp. 59–81. https://doi.org/10.1007/978-3-030-76000-7_4.

Dettwyler, K. A. (1995). A time to wean: The hominid blueprint for the natural age of weaning in modern human populations. In P. Stuart-Macadam &

K. A. Dettwyler, eds., *Breastfeeding: Biocultural Perspectives*. Aldine deGruyter, pp. 75–99.

Dewey, K. G. (2013). The challenge of meeting nutrient needs of infants and young children during the period of complementary feeding: An evolutionary perspective. *The Journal of Nutrition*, **143(12),** 2050–2054. https//doi.org/ 10.3945/jn.113.182527.

Dewey, K. G., & Cohen, R. J. (2007). Does birth spacing affect maternal or child nutritional status? A systematic literature review. *Maternal & Child Nutrition*, **3(3)**, 151–173. https://doi.org/10.1111/j.1740-8709.2007.00092.x.

Draghi-Lorenz, R. (2010). Parental reports of jealousy in early infancy: Growing tensions between evidence and theory. In S. L. Hart & M. Legerstee, eds., *Handbook of Jealousy: Theory, Research, and Multidisciplinary Approaches*. Wiley-Blackwell, pp. 235–266. https//:doi .org/10.1002/9781444323542.

Draghi-Lorenz, R., Reddy, V., & Costall, A. (2001). Rethinking the development of "nonbasic" emotions: A critical review of existing theories. *Developmental Review*, **21(3)**, 263–304. https://doi.org/10.1006/ drev.2000.0524.

Dufour, D. L., & Sauther, M. L. (2002). Comparative and evolutionary dimensions of the energetics of human pregnancy and lactation. *American Journal of Human Biology*, **14**, 584–602. https://doi.org/10.1002/ajhb.10071.

Duntley, J. D. (2015). Adaptations to dangers from humans. In D. M. Buss, ed., *The Handbook of Evolutionary Psychology*. Wiley, pp. 224–257. https://doi.org/10.1002/9780470939376.ch8.

Dyson, T. (1977). Levels, trends, differentials, and causes of child mortality. *World Health Statistics Report*, **30**, 282–311.

Eerkens, J. W., & Bartelink, E. J. (2013). Sex-biased weaning and early childhood diet among middle Holocene hunter-gatherers in Central California. *American Journal of Physical Anthropology*, **152(4)**, 471–483. https://doi.org/10.1002/ajpa.22384.

Eibl-Eibesfeldt, I. (1989). *Human Ethology*. Aldine deGruyter.

Ellis, B. J., & Bjorklund, D. F. (2005). Evolutionary psychology and child development: An emerging synthesis. In B. J. Ellis & D. F. Bjorklund, eds., *Origins of the Social Mind: Evolutionary Psychology and Child Development*. Guilford, pp. 3–17.

Ellison, P. T. (1995). Breastfeeding, fertility, and maternal condition. In P. Stuart-Macadam & K. Dettwyler, eds., *Breastfeeding: Biocultural Perspectives*. Aldine, pp. 305–345.

Emde, R. N., Gaensbauer, R.J. & Harmon, R. J. (1976). Emotional expression in infancy: A biobehavioral study. *Psychological Issues*, **10**, 1–200.

Everett, D. L. (2014). Concentric circles of attachment among the Pirahã: A brief survey. In H. Otto & H. Keller, eds., *Different Faces of Attachment: Cultural Variations on a Universal Human Need*. Cambridge, Cambridge University Press , pp. 169–186.

Emmott, E. H. (2023). *Improving Breastfeeding Rates: Evolutionary Anthropological Insights for Public Health. Cambridge Elements: Elements in Applied Evolutionary Science*. Cambridge University Press. https://doi.org/10.1017/9781009217491.

Emmott, E. H., & Page, A. E. (2019). Alloparenting. In T. K. Shackelford & V. A. Weekes-Shackelford, eds., *Encyclopedia of Evolutionary Psychological Science*. Springer, pp. 1–14. https://doi.org/10.1007/978-3-319-19650-3_2253.

Farroni, T., Della Longa, L., & Valori, I. (2022). The self-regulatory affective touch: A speculative framework for the development of executive functioning. *Current Opinion in Behavioral Sciences*, **43**, 167–173. https://doi.org/10.1016/j.cobeha.2021.10.007.

Feachem, R. G., & Koblinsky, M. A. (1984). Interventions for the control of diarrhoeal diseases among young children: Promotion of breast-feeding. *Bulletin of the World Health Organization*, **62(2),** 271.

Feeny, B. C. & Woodhouse, S. S. (2016). Caregiving. In J. Cassidy & P. R. Shaver, eds., *Handbook of Attachment: Theory, Research and Clinical Applications, 3rd ed.* Guilford, pp. 827–851.

Fernandez, A. M., Acevedo, Y., Baeza, C. G., Dufey, M., & Puga, I. (2022). Jealousy protest to a social rival compared to a nonsocial rival in Chilean infants 10–20 months' old. *Infancy*, **27(5),** 997–1003. https://doi.org/10.1111/infa.12484.

Field, C. (2011). Bowlby's stages of attachment. In S. Goldstein & J. A. Naglieri, eds., *Encyclopedia of Child Behavior and Development*. Springer, pp. 275–277. https://doi.org/10.1007/978-0-387-79061-9_398.

Flensborg, G., Martínez, G., & Bayala, P. D. (2015). Mortality profiles of hunter-gatherer societies: A case study from the eastern Pampa–Patagonia transition (Argentina) during the Final Late Holocene. *International Journal of Osteoarchaeology*, **25(6)**, 816–826. https://doi.org/10.1002/oa.2348.

Fotso, J. C., Cleland, J., Mberu, B., Mutua, M., & Elungata, P. (2013). Birth spacing and child mortality: An analysis of prospective data from the Nairobi urban health and demographic surveillance system. *Journal of Biosocial Science*, **45**, 779–798. https://doi.org/10.1017/S0021932012000570.

Fouts, H. N., & Lamb, M. E. (2005). Weaning emotional patterns among the Bofi Foragers of Central Africa: The role of maternal availability and sensitivity. In B. S. Hewlett & M. E. Lamb, eds., *Hunter-Gatherer Childhoods:*

Evolutionary, Developmental, & Cultural Perspectives. Taylor & Francis, pp. 309–321.

Fouts, H. N., Hewlett, B. S., & Lamb, M. E. (2005). Parent-offspring weaning conflicts among the Bofi farmers and foragers of Central Africa. *Current Anthropology*, **46(1)**, 29–50. https://doi.org/10.1086/425659.

Fox, N. A., Nelson, C. A., & Zeanah, C. H. (2013). The effects of early severe psychosocial deprivation on children's cognitive and social development: Lessons from the Bucharest early intervention project. In N. S. Landsdale, S. M. McHale, & A. Booth, eds., *Families and Child Health*. Springer, pp. 33–41. https://doi.org/10.1007/978-1-4614-6194-4_4.

Freud, A., & Dann, S. (1951). An experiment in group upbringing. *The Psychoanalytic Study of the Child*, **6(1)**, 127–168. https://doi.org/10.1080/00797308.1952.11822909.

Frimpong-Nnuroh, D. (2004). Ghost mothers and wet nurses: Breast feeding practices and care of children in crisis in Ellembelle Nzema. *Institute of African Studies Research Review*, **2004(sup-6)**, 85–92. https://hdl.handle.net/10520/EJC45857.

Galway-Witham, J., & Stringer, C. (2018). How did *Homo sapiens* evolve? *Science*, **360(6395)**, 1296–1298. http://doi.org/10.1126/science.aat665.

Geary, D. C., & Bjorklund, D. F. (2000). Evolutionary developmental psychology. *Child Development*, **71(1)**, 57–65. https://doi.org/10.1111/1467-8624.00258.

Girma, B., Nigussie, J., Molla, A., & Mareg, M. (2022). Under-nutrition and associated factors among lactating mothers in Ethiopia: A systematic review and meta-analysis. *Maternal and Child Health Journal*, **26**, 2210–2220. https://doi.org/10.1007/s10995-022-03467-6.

Gottlieb, A. (2014). Is it time to detach from attachment theory? Perspectives from the West African rain forest. In H. Otto & H. Keller, eds., *Different Faces of Attachment: Cultural Variations on a Universal Human Need*. Cambridge, Cambridge University Press, pp. 187–214.

Gracey, M. (2004). Orphaned and vulnerable to infection, undernutrition and early death: Increasing threats to infants and children. *Acta Pædiatrica*, **93(1)**, 8–9. https://doi.org/10.1111/j.1651-2227.2004.tb00665.x.

Grammatikaki, E., & Huybrechts, I. (2016). Infants: Nutritional requirements. In B. Caballero, P. Finglas, & F. Toldrá, eds., *Encyclopedia of Food and Health*. Amsterdam, Elsevier, pp. 410–416. https://doi.org/10.1007/s13197-020-04384-8.

Gray, S. J. (1996). Ecology of weaning among nomadic Turkana pastoralists of Kenya: Maternal thinking, maternal behavior, and human adaptive strategies. *Human Biology*, **68**, 437–465. www.jstor.org/stable/41465488.

Groucutt, H. S., Petraglia, M. D., Bailey, G. et al. (2015). Rethinking the dispersal of *Homo sapiens* out of Africa. *Evolutionary Anthropology: Issues, News, and Reviews*, **24(4)**, 149–164. https://doi.org/10.1002/evan.21455.

Gunnar, M. (2005). Attachment and stress in early development. In C. S. Carter, L. Ahnert, K. E. Grossman et al., eds., *Attachment and Bonding: A New Synthesis*. MIT Press, pp. 245–255.

Gurven, M. (2004). Reciprocal altruism and food sharing decisions among Hiwi and Ache hunter–gatherers. *Behavioral Ecology and Sociobiology*, *56*, 366–380. https://doi.org/10.1007/s00265-004-0793-6.

Gurven, M., & Kaplan, H. (2007). Longevity among hunter-gatherers: A cross-cultural examination. *Population and Development Review*, **33(2)**, 321–365. https://doi.org/10.1111/j.1728-4457.2007.00171.x.

Guyatt, H., Muiruri, F., Mburu, P., & Robins, A. (2020). Prevalence and predictors of underweight and stunting among children under 2 years of age in Eastern Kenya. *Public Health Nutrition*, **23(9)**, 1599–1608. https://doi.org/10.1017/S1368980019003793.

Hagen, E. H., & Symons, D. (2007). Natural psychology: The environment of evolutionary adaptedness and the structure of cognition. In S. W. Gangestad & J. A. Simpson, eds., *The Evolution of Mind: Fundamental Questions and Controversies*. Guilford Press, pp. 38–43.

Hailemariam, A., & Tesfaye, M. (1997). Determinants of infant and early childhood mortality in a small urban community of Ethiopia: A hazard model analysis. *Ethiopian Journal of Health Development*, **11(3)**, 189–200.

Hardin, J. S., Jones, N. A., Mize, K. D., & Platt, M. (2020). Parent-training with kangaroo care impacts infant neurophysiological development & mother-infant neuroendocrine activity. *Infant Behavior and Development*, **58**, 101416. https://doi.org/10.1016/j.infbeh.2019.101416.

Harkness, S., & Super, C. M. (2002). Culture and parenting. In M. C. Bornstein, ed., *Handbook of Parenting: Biology and Ecology of Parenting*. Erlbaum, pp. 253–280.

Harlow, H. F. (1958). The nature of love. *American Psychologist*, **13**, 673–685. https://psycnet.apa.org/doi/10.1037/h0047884.

Hart, S. L. (2010). The ontogenesis of jealousy in the first year of life: A theory of jealousy as a biologically-based dimension of temperament. In S. L. Hart & M. Legerstee, eds., *Handbook of Jealousy: Theory, Research, and Multidisciplinary Approaches*. Wiley-Blackwell, pp. 58–82. https://doi.org/10.1002/9781444323542.

Hart, S. L. (2015). *Jealousy in Infants: Laboratory Research on Differential Treatment*. Springer.

Hart, S. L. (2016a). Jealousy protest: Ontogeny in accord with the 9-month period of human gestation. *Evolutionary Psychology*, **14**, 1–9. https://doi.org/10.1177/1474704916646.

Hart, S. L. (2016b). Proximal foundations of jealousy: Expectations of exclusivity in the infant's first year of life. *Emotion Review*, **8(4)**, 358–366. https://doi.org/10.1177/1754073915615431.

Hart, S. L. (2018). Jealousy *and* attachment: Adaptations to threat posed by the birth of a sibling. *Evolutionary Behavioral Sciences*, **12**, 263–275. https://doi.org/10.1037/ebs0000102.

Hart, S. L. (2022a). Attachment and caregiving in the ancestral mother-infant dyad: Evolutionary developmental psychology models of their origins in the environment of evolutionary adaptedness. In S. L. Hart & D. F. Bjorklund, eds., *Evolutionary Perspectives on Infancy*. Springer, pp. 135–160. https://doi.org/10.1007/978-3-030-76000-7_7.

Hart, S. L. (2022b). Jealousy and the terrible twos. In S. L. Hart & D. F. Bjorklund, eds., *Evolutionary Perspectives on Infancy*. Springer, pp. 325–347. https://doi.org/10.1007/978-3-030-76000-7_15.

Hart, S. L., & Behrens, K. Y. (2013a). Affective and behavioral features of jealousy protest: Associations with child temperament, maternal interaction style, and attachment. *Infancy*, **18**, 369–399. https://doi.org/10.1111/j.1532-7078.2012.00123.x.

Hart, S. L., & Behrens, K. Y. (2013b). Regulation of jealousy protest in the context of reunion following differential treatment. *Infancy*, **18**, 1076–1110. https://doi.org/10.1111/infa.12024

Hart, S. L., & Carrington, H. (2002). Jealousy in 6-month-old infants. *Infancy*, **3**, 395–402. https://doi.org/10.1207/S15327078IN0303_6.

Hart, S. L., Carrington, H. A., Tronick, E. Z., & Carroll, S. R. (2004). When infants lose exclusive maternal attention: Is it jealousy? *Infancy*, **6**, 57–78. https://doi.org/10.1207/s15327078in0601_3.

Hart, S. L., Field, T., Del Valle, C., & Letourneau, M. (1998a). Infants protest their mothers' attending to an infant-size baby doll. *Social Development*, **7**, 54–61. https://doi.org/10.1111/1467-9507.00050.

Hart, S., Field, T., Letourneau, M., & Del Valle, C. (1998b). Jealousy protests in infants of depressed mothers. *Infant Behavior and Development*, **21(1)**, 137–148. https://doi.org/10.1016/S0163-6383(98)90059-5.

Hart, S., Jones, N. A., & Field, T. (2003). Atypical expressions of jealousy in infants of intrusive- and withdrawn-depressed mothers. *Child Psychiatry and Human Development*, **33**, 193–207. https://doi.org/10.1023/A:1021452529762.

Hawks, J., Hunley, K., Lee, S.H., & Wolpoff, M. (2000). Population bottlenecks and Pleistocene human evolution. *Molecular Biology and Evolution*, **17(1)**, 2–22. https://doi.org/10.1093/oxfordjournals.molbev.a026233.

He, J., Degnan, K. A., McDermott, J. M. et al. (2010). Anger and approach motivation in infancy: Relations to early childhood inhibitory control and behavior problems. *Infancy*, **15**, 246–269. https://doi.org/10.1111/j.1532-7078.2009.00017.x.

Henry, P. Ivey. , & Morelli, G. A. (2022). Niche construction in hunter-gatherer infancy: Growth and health trade-offs inform social agency. In S. L. Hart & D. F. Bjorklund, eds., *Evolutionary Perspectives on Infancy.* Springer, pp. 213–236. https://doi.org/10.1007/978-3-030-76000-7_10.

Heinicke, C. M. (1956). Some effects of separating two-year-old children from their parents: A comparative study. *Human Relations*, **9(2)**, 105–176. https://doi.org/10.1177/001872675600900201.

Hewlett, B. S., & Winn, S. (2014). Allomaternal nursing in humans. *Current Anthropology*, **55**, 200–229. https://doi.org/10.1086/675657.

Hill, K. R., Walker, R. S., Božičević, M., Eder, J., Headland, T., Hewlett, B., … & Wood, B. (2011). Co-residence patterns in hunter-gatherer societies show unique human social structure. *Science*, *331*(6022), 1286–1289. http://doi:10.1126/science.1199071.

Hinde, K. (2014). Essential tensions in infant rearing. *Evolution, Medicine, and Public Health*, **2014**, 48–50. https://doi.org/10.1093/emph/eou007.

Hinde, K., & Milligan, L. A. (2011). Primate milk: Proximate mechanisms and ultimate perspectives. *Evolutionary Anthropology*, **20(1)**, 9–23. https://doi.org/10.1002/evan.20289.

Hirschman, C. (1979). *Trends in Breast Feeding Among American Mothers.* United States Department of Health, Education, and Welfare, DHEW Publication No. PHS 79-1979.

Hoehn, T., & Hoppenz, M. (2009). Neonatal and childhood mortality rates in Myanmar. *Klinische Pädiatrie*, **221(4)**, 266–268. https://doi.org/1010.1055/s-0029-1220904.

Howcroft, R., Eriksson, G., & Lidén, K. (2012). The milky way: The implications of using animal milk products in infant feeding. *Anthropozoologica*, **47(2)**, 31–43. https://doi.org/10.5252/az2012n2a3.

Howes, C., & Spieker, S. (2008). Attachment relationships in the context of multiple caregivers. In J. Cassidy & P. Shaver, eds., *The Handbook of Attachment: Theory, Research, and Clinical Applications*, 2nd ed. Guilford, pp. 317–32.

Hoyle, B., Yunus, M. D., & Chen, L. C. (1980). Breast-feeding and food intake among children with acute diarrheal disease. *The American Journal of Clinical Nutrition*, **33(11)**, 2365–2371. https://doi.org/10.1093/ajcn/33.11.2365.

Hrdy, S. B. (1994). Fitness tradeoffs in the history of evolution of delegating mothering with special reference to wet-nursing, abandonment and infanticide. In S. Parmigiani & F. S. vom Saal, eds., *Infanticide and Parental Care.* Routledge, pp. 3–42.

Hrdy, S. B. (1999). *Mother Nature: Maternal Instincts and How They Shaped the Human Species*. Ballantine.

Hrdy, S. B. (2001). *Mother Nature: A History of Mothers, Infants, and Natural Selection*. Pantheon Books.

Hrdy, S. B. (2007). Evolutionary context of human development: The cooperative breeding model. In C. A. Salmon & T. K. Shackelford, eds., *Family Relationships: An Evolutionary Perspective*. Oxford, pp. 39–68.

Hrdy, S. B. (2009). *Mothers and Others: The Evolutionary Origins of Mutual Understanding*. Press of Harvard University.

Burkart, J. M., Hrdy, S. B., & Van Schaik, C. P. (2009). Cooperative breeding and human cognitive evolution. *Evolutionary Anthropology*, **18**, 175–186. https://doi.org/10.1002/evan.20222.

Hrdy, S. B., & Burkart, J. M. (2022). How reliance on allomaternal care shapes primate development with special reference to the genus homo. In S. L. Hart & D. F. Bjorklund, eds., *Evolutionary Perspectives on Infancy*. Springer, pp. 161–188. https://doi.org/10.1007/978-3-030-76000-7_8.

Hrvoj-Mihic, B., Bienvenu, T., Stefanacci, L., Muotri, A. R., & Semendeferi, K. (2013). Evolution, development, and plasticity of the human brain: From molecules to bones. *Frontiers in Human Neuroscience*, **7**, 1–18. https://doi.org/10.3389/fnhum.2013.00707.

Hss, A. S., Tan, P. S., & Hashim, L. (2014). Childhood drowning in Malaysia. *International Journal of Injury Control and Safety Promotion*, **21(1)**, 75–80. https://doi.org/10.1080/17457300.2013.792284.

Huffman, S. L., & Combest, C. (1990). Role of breast-feeding in the prevention and treatment of diarrhoea. *Journal of Diarrhoeal Diseases Research*, **8**, 68–81. www.jstor.org/stable/23498066.

Humphrey, L. T. (2010). Weaning behaviour in human evolution. *Seminars in Cell & Developmental Biology*, **21**, 453–461. https://doi.org/10.1016/j.semcdb.2009.11.003.

Ionio, C., Ciuffo, G., & Landoni, M. (2021). Parent–infant skin-to-skin contact and stress regulation: A systematic review of the literature. *International Journal of Environmental Research and Public Health*, **18(9)**, 4695. https://doi.org/10.3390/ijerph18094695.

Jansen, P. W., de Barse, L. M., Jaddoe, V. W. et al. (2017). Bi-directional associations between child fussy eating and parents' pressure to eat: Who influences whom? *Physiology & Behavior*, **176**, 101–106. https://doi.org/10.1016/j.physbeh.2017.02.015.

John, C. C., Black, M. M., & Nelson III, C. A. (2017). Neurodevelopment: The impact of nutrition and inflammation during early to middle childhood in low-resource settings. *Pediatrics*, **139 (Supplement_1)**, S59–S71. https://doi.org/10.1542/peds.2016-2828H.

Jakobsen, M. S., Sodemann, M., Mølbak, K. et al. (2003). Termination of breastfeeding after 12 months of age due to a new pregnancy and other causes is associated with increased mortality in Guinea-Bissau. *International Journal of Epidemiology*, **32(1)**, 92–96. https://doi.org/10.1093/ije/dyg006.

Kagan, J. (1976). Emergent themes in human development: Some basic assumptions about the development of cognitive and affective structures and their stability from infancy to later childhood are reexamined in light of new evidence from a variety of sources. *American Scientist*, **64(2)**, 186–196. www.jstor.org/stable/27847159.

Kagan, J., Kearsley, R. B., & Zelazo, P. R. (1980). *Infancy, Its Place in Human Development*. Harvard University Press.

Kamal, V. K., Srivastav, S., Kumari, D., & Ranjan, M. (2020). Identification of distinct risk subsets for under-five mortality in India using CART model: An evidence from NFHS-4. *Journal of Global Health Reports*, *4*, **e2020055**. https://doi.org/10.29392/001c.13169.

Kaplan, H. S., & Robson, A. J. (2002). The emergence of humans: The coevolution of intelligence and longevity with intergenerational transfers. *Proceedings of the National Academy of Sciences*, **99(15)**, 10221–10226. https://doi.org/10.1073/pnas.152502899.

Kardulias, P. N. (2018). Migration of *Homo sapiens* out of Africa. In E. Chiotis, ed.,*Climate Changes in the Holocene*: *Impacts and Human* Adaptation. CRC Press, pp. 143–155.

Kassaw, A., Amare, D., Birhanu, M., et al. (2021). Survival and predictors of mortality among severe acute malnourished under-five children admitted at Felege-Hiwot comprehensive specialized hospital, northwest, Ethiopia: A retrospective cohort study. *BMC Pediatrics*, **21(1)**, 1–10. https://doi.org/10.1186/s12887-021-02651-x.

Kearsley, R. B., Hartmann, R., Zelazo, P. R., & Kagan, J. (1975). Separation protest in day-care and home-reared infants. *Pediatrics*, **55(2)**, 171–175. https://doi.org/10.1542/peds.55.2.171.

Keller, H., & Otto, H. (2014). Epilogue: The future of attachment. In H. Otto & H. Keller, eds., *Different Faces of Attachment: Cultural Variations on a Universal Human Need*. Cambridge, Cambridge University Press, pp. 307–312.

Khan, J., & Das, S. K. (2020). The burden of anthropometric failure and child mortality in India. *Scientific Reports*, **10(1)**, 1–16. https://doi.org/10.1038/s41598-020-76884-8.

Kimminau, D. (2021). Weaning. In T. K. Shackelford & V. A. Weekes-Shackelford, eds., *Encyclopedia of Evolutionary Psychological Science*. Springer, pp. 8486–8490. https://doi.org/10.1007/978-3-319-19650-3_837.

Koenig, M. A., Phillips, J. F., Campbell, O. M., & D'Souza, S. (1990). Birth intervals and childhood mortality in rural Bangladesh. *Demography*, **27(2)**, 251–265. https://doi.org/10.2307/2061452.

Kominiarek, M. A., & Rajan, P. (2016). Nutrition recommendations in pregnancy and lactation. *Medical Clinics*, **100(6)**, 1199–1215. https://doi.org/10.1016/j.mcna.2016.06.004.

Konner, M. (2005). Hunter-gatherer infancy and childhood: The !Kung and others. In B. S. Hewlett & M. E. Lamb, eds., *Hunter-Gatherer Childhoods: Evolutionary, Developmental, and Cultural Perspectives*. Routledge, pp. 19–64.

Konner, M. (2018). Nonmaternal care: A half-century of research. *Physiology & Behavior*, **193**, 179–186. https://doi.org/10.1016/j.physbeh.2018.03.025.

Kramer, K. L. (2019). How there got to be so many of us: The evolutionary story of population growth and a life history of cooperation. *Journal of Anthropological Research*, **75(4)**, 472–497. https://doi.org/10.1086/705943.

Küpers, L. K., L'Abée, C., Bocca, G. et al. (2015). Determinants of weight gain during the first two years of life—the GECKO Drenthe birth cohort. *PLoS One*, **10(7)**, e0133326. https://doi.org/10.1371/journal.pone.0133326.

Lamberti, L. M., Zakarija-Grković, I., Fischer Walker, C. L. et al. (2013). Breastfeeding for reducing the risk of pneumonia morbidity and mortality in children under two: A systematic literature review and meta-analysis. *BMC Public Health*, **13(3)**, 1–8. https://doi.org/10.1186/1471-2458-13-S3-S18.

Lancy, D. F. (2008). *The Anthropology of Childhood: Cherubs, Chattel, Changelings*. Cambridge University Press.

Lee, R. B. (1976). Introduction. In R. B. Lee & I. DeVore, eds., *Kalahari Hunter-Gatherers: Studies of the !Kung San and their Neighbors*. Harvard University Press, pp. 3–24. https://doi.org/10.4159/harvard.9780674430600.

Lawrence, R. A. (2022). Induced lactation and relactation (including nursing an adopted baby) and cross-nursing. In R. A. Lawrence & R. M. Lawrence, eds., *Breastfeeding, A Guide for Medical Professionals*, 9th ed. Elsevier, pp. 628–45. https://doi.org/10.1016/B978-0-323-68013-4.00019-5.

LeVine, R. A. (2014). Attachment theory as cultural ideology. In H. Otto & H. Keller, eds., *Different Faces of Attachment: Cultural Variations on a Universal Human Need*. Cambridge, Cambridge University Press, pp. 50–65.

Levy, D. M. (1934). Rivalry between children in the same family. *Child Study*, **11**, 233–239.

Levy, D. M. (1937). Studies in sibling rivalry. *Research Monographs of the American Orthopsychiatric Association*, **2**, 1–96.

Lester, B. M., Kotelchuch, M., Spelke, E., Sellers, M. J., & Klein, R. E. (1974). Separation protest in Guatemalan infants: Cross-cultural and cognitive findings. *Developmental Psychology*, **10(1)**, 79–85. https://psycnet.apa.org/doi/10.1037/h0035562.

Linnan, M., Giersing, M., Cox, R. et al. (2007). *Child Mortality and Injury in Asia: An overview, Innocenti Working Paper 2007-04, Special Series on Child Injury No. 1.* UNICEF Innocenti Research Centre.

Liu, L., Oza, S., Hogan, D. et al. (2015). Global, regional, and national causes of child mortality in 2000–13, with projections to inform post-2015 priorities: An updated systematic analysis. *The Lancet*, **385(9966)**, 430–440. https://doi.org/10.1016/S0140-6736(14)61698-6.

LoBue, V., & Rakison, D. H. (2013). What we fear most: A developmental advantage for threat-relevant stimuli. *Developmental Review*, **33(4)**, 285–303. https://doi.org/10.1016/j.dr.2013.07.005.

Locke, J. L., & Bogin, B. (2022). An unusually human time: Effects of the most social stage on the most social species. In S. L. Hart & D. F. Bjorklund, eds., *Evolutionary Perspectives on Infancy.* Springer, pp. 107–133. https://doi.org/10.1007/978-3-030-76000-7_6.

López-Fernández, G., Barrios, M., Goberna-Tricas, J., & Gómez-Benito, J. (2017). Breastfeeding during pregnancy: A systematic review. *Women and Birth*, **30(6)**, e292–e300. https://doi.org/10.1016/j.wombi.2017.05.008.

Loponte, D., & Mazza, B. (2021). Breastfeeding and weaning in Late Holocene hunter-gatherers of the lower Paraná wetland, South America. *American Journal of Physical Anthropology*, **176(3)**, 504–520. https://doi.org/10.1002/ajpa.24381.

Luby, J. L., Belden, A. C., Pautsch, J., Si, X., & Spitznagel, E. (2009). The clinical significance of preschool depression: Impairment in functioning and clinical markers of the disorder. *Journal of Affective Disorders*, **112(1–3)**, 111–119. https://doi.org/10.1016/j.jad.2008.03.026.

Mackes, N. K. Golm, D., Sarkar, S. et al. (2020). Early childhood deprivation is associated with alterations in adult brain structure despite subsequent environmental enrichment. *Proceedings of the National Academy of Sciences*, **117(1)**, 641–649. https://doi.org/10.1073/pnas.1911264116.

Mannino, M. A., Thomas, K. D., Leng, M. J., Di Salvo, R., & Richards, M. P. (2011). Stuck to the shore? Investigating prehistoric hunter-gatherer subsistence, mobility, and territoriality in a Mediterranean coastal landscape through isotope analyses on marine mollusc shell carbonates and human bone collagen. *Quaternary International*, **244(1)**, 88–104. https://doi.org/10.1016/j.quaint.2011.05.044.

Martin, M. (2017). Mixed-feeding in humans: Evolution and current implications.In M. Martin, ed., *Breastfeeding: New Anthropological Approaches.* Routledge, pp. 140–154. https://doi.10.4324/9781315145129-10.

Masmas, T. N., Jensen, H., Da Silva, D. et al. (2004). Survival among motherless children in rural and urban areas in Guinea-Bissau. *Acta Paediatrica*, **93(1)**, 99–105. https://doi.org/10.1111/j.1651-2227.2004.tb00682.x.

McDade, T. W., & Worthman, C. M. (1998). The weanling's dilemma reconsidered: A biocultural analysis of breastfeeding ecology. *Journal of Developmental and Behavioral Pediatrics*, **19**, 286–299. https://doi.org/10.1097/00004703-199808000-00008.

McDowell, H., & Volk, A. A. (2022). Infant mortality. In S. L. Hart & D. F. Bjorklund, eds., *Evolutionary Perspectives on Infancy*. Springer, pp. 83–103. https://doi.org/10.1097/00004703-199808000-00008.

McKenna, J. J., Thoman, E. B., Anders, T. F. et al. (1993). Infant—parent co-sleeping in an evolutionary perspective: Implications for understanding infant sleep development and the sudden infant death syndrome. *Sleep*, **16 (3)**, 263–282. https://doi.org/10.1093/sleep/16.3.263.

Meehan, C. L., & Hawks, S. (2014). Maternal and allomaternal responsiveness: Allomothering, stranger anxiety, and intimacy. In H. Otto & H. Keller, eds., *Different Faces of Attachment: Cultural Variations on a Universal Human Need*. Cambridge, Cambridge University Press, pp. 113–140.

Meek, J. Y., & Noble, L. (2022). Policy statement: Breastfeeding and the use of human milk. *Pediatrics*, **150(1)**, **e2022057988**. https://doi.org/10.1542/peds.2022-057988.

Mikulincer, M., & Shaver, P. R. (2019). Attachment, caregiving, and parenting. In O. Taubman – Ben-Ari, ed., *Pathways and Barriers to Parenthood: Existential Concerns Regarding Fertility, Pregnancy, and Early Parenthood*. Springer, pp. 305–319. https://doi.org/10.1007/978-3-030-24864-2_18.

Mize, K. D., & Jones, N. A. (2012). Infant physiological and behavioral responses to loss of maternal attention to a social-rival. *International Journal of Psychophysiology*, **83**, 16–23. https://doi.org/10.1016/j.ijpsycho.2011.09.018.

Mize, K. D., Pineda, M., Blau, A. K., Marsh, K., & Jones, N. A. (2014). Infant physiological and behavioral responses to a jealousy provoking condition. *Infancy*, **19**, 338–348. https://doi.org/10.1111/infa.12046.

Moberg, K. U., Handlin, L., & Petersson, M. (2020). Neuroendocrine mechanisms involved in the physiological effects caused by skin-to-skin contact–With a particular focus on the oxytocinergic system. *Infant Behavior and Development*, **61**, 101482. https://doi.org/10.1016/j.infbeh.2020.101482.

Moberg, K. U., & Petersson, M. (2022). Physiological effects induced by stimulation of cutaneous sensory nerves, with a focus on oxytocin. *Current Opinion in Behavioral Sciences*, **43**, 159–166. https://doi.org/10.1016/j.cobeha.2021.10.001.

Molitoris, J. (2019). Breast-feeding during pregnancy and the risk of miscarriage. *Perspectives on Sexual and Reproductive Health*, **51(3)**, 153–163. https://doi.org/10.1363/psrh.12120.

Moore, E. R., Bergman, N., Anderson, G. C., & Medley, N. (2016). Early skin-to-skin contact for mothers and their healthy newborn infants. *Cochrane Database of Systematic Reviews*, **(11)**. https://doi.org/10.1002/14651858.CD003519.pub4.

Mozumder, A. B. M. K. A., Kane, T. T., Levin, A., & Ahmed, S. (2000). The effect of birth interval on malnutrition in Bangladeshi infants and young children. *Journal of Biosocial Science*, **32(3)**, 289–300. https://doi.org/10.1017/S0021932000002893.

Murphy, T. P., McCurdy, K., Jehl, B., Rowan, M., & Larrimore, K. (2020). Jealousy behaviors in early childhood: Associations with attachment and temperament. *International Journal of Behavioral Development*, **44(3)**, 266–272. https://doi.org/10.1177/0165025419877974.

Narayan, J., John, D., & Ramadas, N. (2019). Malnutrition in India: Status and government initiatives. *Journal of Public Health Policy*, **40(1)**, 126–141. https://doi.org/10.1057/s41271-018-0149-5.

Narvaez, D., Gray, P., McKenna, J. J., Fuentes, A., & Valentino, K. (2014). Children's development in light of evolution and culture. In D. Narvaez, K. Valentino, A. Fuentes, & J. J. McKenna, eds., *Ancestral Landscapes in Human Evolution: Culture, Childrearing, and Social Wellbeing*. Oxford, Oxford University Press, pp. 3–17.

Norholt, H. (2020). Revisiting the roots of attachment: A review of the biological and psychological effects of maternal skin-to-skin contact and carrying of full-term infants. *Infant Behavior and Development*, **60**, 101441. https://doi.org/10.1016/j.infbeh.2020.101441.

Osborne, A. H., Vance, D., Rohling, E. J. et al. (2008). A humid corridor across the Sahara for the migration of early modern humans out of Africa 120,000 years ago. *Proceedings of the National Academy of Sciences*, **105(43)**, 16444–16447. https://doi.org/10.1073/pnas.0804472105.

Pauen, S., & Hoehl, S. (2015). Preparedness to learn about the world: Evidence from infant research. In T. Breyer, ed., *Epistemological Dimensions of Evolutionary Psychology*. Springer, pp. 159–173. https://doi.org/10.1007/978-1-4939-1387-9_8.

Pontzer, H., Wood, B. M., & Raichlen, D. A. (2018). Hunter-gatherers as models in public health. *Obesity Reviews*, **19**, 24–35. https://doi.org/10.1111/obr.12785.

Prado, E. L., & Dewey, K. G. (2014). Nutrition and brain development in early life. *Nutrition Reviews*, **72(4)**, 267–284. https://doi.org/10.1111/nure.12102,

Praetorius, S. K., Alder, J. R., Condron, A. et al. (2023). Ice and ocean constraints on early human migrations into North America along the Pacific coast. *Proceedings of the National Academy of Sciences*, **120(7)**, e2208738120. https://doi.org/10.1073/pnas.2208738120.

Quinlan, R. J., Quinlan, M. B., & Flinn, M. V. (2003). Parental investment and age at weaning in a Caribbean village. *Evolution and Human Behavior*, **24(1)**, 1–16. https://doi.org/10.1016/S1090-5138(02)00104-6.

Quinn, E. A. (2016). Infancy by design: Maternal metabolism, hormonal signals, and the active management of infant growth by human milk. In W. R. Trevathan & K. R. Rosenberg, eds., *Costly and Cute: Helpless Infants and Human Evolution*. School for Advanced Research, pp. 87–107.

Rakison, D. H. (2022). Fear learning in infancy: An evolutionary developmental perspective. In S. L. Hart & D. F. Bjorklund, eds., *Evolutionary Perspectives on Infancy*. Springer, pp. 303–324. https://doi.org/10.1007/978-3-030-76000-7_14.

Rakison, D. H., & Derringer, J. (2008). Do infants possess an evolved spider-detection mechanism? *Cognition*, **107(1)**, 381–393. https://doi.org/10.1016/j.cognition.2007.07.022.

Rahman, M. M., Kabir, M., & Amin, R. (1996). Relationship between survival status of first child and subsequent child death. *Journal of Biosocial Science*, **28(2)**, 185–191. https://doi.org/10.1017/S0021932000022239.

Ramani, K. V., Mavalankar, D., Joshi, S. et al. (2010). Why should 5,000 children die in India every day? Major causes of death and managerial challenges. *Vikalpa*, **35(2)**, 9–20. https://doi.org/10.1177/0256090920100202.

Ray, S. K. (2011). Evidence-based preventive interventions for targeting under-nutrition in the Indian context. *Indian Journal of Public Health*, **55(1)**, 1–6. https://doi.org/10.4103/0019-557X.82531.

Razzaque, A., Da Vanzo, J., Rahman, M. et al. (2005). Pregnancy spacing and maternal morbidity in Matlab, Bangladesh. *International Journal of Gynecology & Obstetrics*, **89**, S41–S49. https://doi.org/10.1016/j.ijgo.2005.01.003.

Ronsmans, C. (1996). Birth spacing and child survival in rural Senegal. *International Journal of Epidemiology*, **25(5)**, 989–997. https://doi.org/10.1093/ije/25.5.989.

Saloojee, H., & Pettifor, J. M. (2005). International child health: 10 years of democracy in South Africa; The challenges facing children today. *Current Paediatrics*, **15(5)**, 429–436. https://doi.org/10.1016/j.cupe.2005.06.012.

Salmon, C., & Hehman, J. (2022). Evolutionary perspectives on mother-infant conflict. In S. L. Hart & D. F. Bjorklund, eds., *Evolutionary Perspectives on Infancy*, Springer, pp. 189–211. https://doi.org/10.1007/978-3-030-76000-7_9.

Salmon, M. (1994). The cultural significance of breastfeeding and infant care in early America. *Journal of Social History*, **28**, 247–269. www.jstor.org/stable/ 3788897.

Salmon, C., & Hehman, J. (2022). Evolutionary perspectives on infant-mother conflict. In S. L. Hart & D. F. Bjorklund, eds., *Evolutionary Perspectives on Infancy*. Springer, pp. 189–211. https://doi.org/10.1007/978-3-030-76000-7_9.

Scanes, C. G. (2018). Hunter-gatherers. In C. G. Scanes & S. R. Toukhsati, eds., *Animals and Human Society*. Elsevier, pp. 65–82.

Shachar, B. Z., & Lyell, D. J. (2012). Interpregnancy interval and obstetrical complications. *Obstetrical & Gynecological Survey*, **67(9)**, 584–596. https:// doi.org/10.1097/OGX.0b013e31826b2c3e.

Scrimshaw, S. C. M. (1984). Infanticide in human populations: Societal and individual concerns. In G. Hausfater & S. B. Hrdy, eds., *Infanticide: Comparative and Evolutionary Perspectives*. Aldine, pp. 439–462.

Seaman, J. (1972). Relief work in a refugee camp for Bangladesh refugees in India. *The Lancet*, **300**, 866–870. https://doi.org/10.1016/S0140-6736(72) 92225-8.

Sear, R., & Mace, R. (2008). Who keeps children alive? A review of the effects of kin on child survival. *Evolution and Human Behavior*, **29(1)**, 1–18. https:// doi.org/10.1016/j.evolhumbehav.2007.10.001.

Sellen, D. W., & Smay, D. B. (2001). Relationship between subsistence and age at weaning in "preindustrial" societies. *Human Nature*, **12**, 47–87. https://doi.org/10.1007/s12110-001-1013-y.

Sengül, O., Sivaslıoğlu, A. A., Kokanali, M. K., Ustüner, I., & Avşar, A. F. (2013). The outcomes of the pregnancies of lactating women. *Turkish Journal of Medical Sciences*, **43(2)**, 251–254. https://doi.org/10.3906/sag-1207-33.

Shaaban, O. M., Abbas, A. M., Hafiz, H. A. et al. (2015). Effect of pregnancy-lactation overlap on the current pregnancy outcome in women with substandard nutrition: A prospective cohort study. *Facts, Views & Vision in ObGyn*, **7(4)**, 213–221.

Shannon, K., Mahmud, Z., Asfia, A., & Ali, M. (2008). The social and environ-mental factors underlying maternal malnutrition in rural Bangladesh: Implications for reproductive health and nutrition programs. *Health Care for Women International*, **29(8–9)**, 826–840. https://doi.org/10.1080/ 07399330802269493.

Shostak, M. (1976). A !Kung woman's memories of childhood. In R. B. Lee & I. De Vore, eds., *Kalahari Hunter-Gatherers: Studies of the !Kung San and their Neighbors*. Harvard University Press, pp. 246–277. https://doi.org/ 10.4159/harvard.9780674430600.c18.

Silk, J. B. (2007). Who lived in the environment of evolutionary adaptedness? In S. W. Gangestad & J. A. Simpson, eds., *The Evolution of Mind: Fundamental Questions and Controversies*. Guilford Press, pp. 103–110.

Smith, T. M. (2013). Teeth and human life-history evolution. *Annual Review of Anthropology*, **42**, 191–208. www.annualreviews.org/doi/full/10.1146/annurev-an-42.

Sonuga-Barke, E. J. S., Kennedy, M., Kumsta, R. et al. (2017). Child-to-adult neurodevelopmental and mental health trajectories after early life deprivation: The young adult follow-up of the longitudinal English and Romanian Adoptees study. *Lancet*, **389**, 1539–1548. https://doi.org/10.1016/S0140-6736(17)30045-4.

Spitz, R. A. (1945). Hospitalism: An inquiry into the genesis of psychiatric conditions in early childhood. *The Psychoanalytic Study of the Child*, **1**, 53–74. http://doi:10.1080/00797308.1945.11823126.

Spitz, R. A. (1949). The role of ecological factors in emotional development in infancy. *Child Development*, **20**, 145–155. https://doi.org/10.2307/1125870.

Stanton, J. (2001). Listening to the Ga: Cicely Williams' discovery of kwashiorkor on the Gold Coast. In A. Hardy & L. Conrad, eds., *Women and Modern Medicine*. Brill, pp. 149–171. https://doi.org/10.1163/9789004333390_008.

Stuart-Macadam, P. (1995). Breastfeeding in prehistory. In P. Stuart-Macadam & K. Dettwyler, eds., *Breastfeeding: Biocultural Perspectives*. Aldine deGruyter, pp. 75–99.

Super, C. M., Guldan, G. S., Ahmed, N., & Zeitlin, M. (2012). The emergence of separation protest is robust under conditions of severe developmental stress in rural Bangladesh. *Infant Behavior and Development*, **35(3)**, 393–396. https://doi.org/10.1016/j.infbeh.2012.02.010.

Szabó, N., Dubas, J. S., & van Aken, M. A. (2014). Jealousy in firstborn toddlers within the context of the primary family triad. *Social Development*, **23(2)**, 325–339. https://doi.org/10.1111/sode.12039.

Taylor, M. K., & Kogan, K. L. (1973). Effects of birth of a sibling on mother-child interactions. *Child Psychiatry and Human Development*, **4(1)**, 53–58. https://doi.org/10.1007/BF01434184.

Tessone, A., García Guraieb, S., Goñi, R. A., & Panarello, H. O. (2015). Isotopic evidence of weaning in hunter-gatherers from the Late Holocene in Lake Salitroso, Patagonia, Argentina. *American Journal of Physical Anthropology*, **158(1)**, 105–115. https://doi.org/10.1002/ajpa.22768.

Teti, D. M., Sakin, J. W., Kucera, E., Corns, K. M., & Eiden, R. D. (1996). And baby makes four: Predictors of attachment security among preschool-age firstborns during the transition to siblinghood. *Child Development*, **67(2)**, 579–596. https://doi.org/10.1111/j.1467-8624.1996.tb01752.x.

Thoman, E. B. (2006). Co-sleeping, an ancient practice: Issues of the past and present, and possibilities for the future. *Sleep Medicine Reviews*, **10**, 407–417. https://doi.org/10.1016/j.smrv.2005.12.001.

Tooby, J. & Cosmides, L. (1992). The psychological foundations of culture. In J. Barkow, L. Cosmides & J. Tooby, eds., *The Adapted Mind: Evolutionary Psychology and the Generation of Culture*. Oxford University Press, pp. 19–136.

Touris M., Kromelow S., & Harding C. (1995). Mother-firstborn attachment and the birth of a sibling. *American Journal of Orthopsychiatry*, **65**, 293–297. https://doi:10.1037/h0079614.

Trivers, R. L. (1974). Parent-offspring conflict. *American Zoologist*, **14**, 249–264. https://doi.org/10.1093/icb/14.1.249.

Truswell, A. S. & Hansen, J. D. L. (1976). Medical research among the !Kung. In R. B. Lee & I. DeVore, eds., *Kalahari Hunter-Gatherers: Studies of the !Kung San and their Neighbors*. Harvard University Press, pp. 166–194. https://ehrafworldcultures.yale.edu/document?id=fx10-048.

Troeger, C., Blacker, B., Khalil, I. A. et al. (2018). Estimates of the global, regional and national morbidity, mortality and aetiologies of lower respiratory infections in 195 countries, 1990–2016: A systematic analysis for the global burden of disease study 2016. *The Lancet Infectious Diseases*, **18(11)**, 1191–1210. https://doi.org/10.1016/S1473-3099(18)30310-4.

Tronick, E., Als, H., Adamson, L., Wise, S., & Brazelton, T. B. (1978). The infant's response to entrapment between contradictory messages in face-to-face interaction. *Journal of the American Academy of Child Psychiatry*, **17 (1)**, 1–13. https://doi.org/10.1016/S0002-7138(09)62273-1.

Tronick, E. Z., Morelli, G. A., & Winn, S. (1989). The caretaker-child strategic model: Efe and Aka child rearing as exemplars of the multiple factors affecting child rearing-A reply to Hewlett. *American Anthropologist*, **91(1)**, 192–194. www.jstor.org/stable/679754.

Tronick, E. Z., Morelli, G. A., & Ivey, P. K. (1992). The Efe forager infant and toddler's pattern of social relationships: Multiple and simultaneous. *Developmental Psychology*, **28**, 568–577. www.jstor.org/stable/679754.

Ubesie, A. C., Ibeziako, N. S., Ndiokwelu, C. I., Uzoka, C. M., & Nwafor, C. A. (2012). Under-five protein energy malnutrition admitted at the University of in Nigeria teaching hospital, Enugu: A 10 year retrospective review. *Nutrition Journal*, **11(1)**, 1–7. https://doi.org/10.1186/1475-2891-11-43.

Udipi, S. A., Ghugre, P., & Antony, U. (2000). Nutrition in pregnancy and lactation. *Journal of the Indian Medical Association*, **98(9)**, 548–557.

UNICEF (2019). The State of the World's Children, 2019. Children, Food and Nutrition: Growing Well in a Changing World. www.unicef.org/reports/state-of-worlds-children-2019 (Accessed February 28, 2023).

UNICEF (2023). First 1000 Days. www.unicef.org/southafrica/media/551/file/ZAF-First-1000-days-brief-2017.pdf (Accessed February 28, 2023).

United Nations (2015). *The Millennium Development Goals Report, 2015.* www.un.org/millenniumgoals/2015_MDG_Report/pdf/MDG%202015%20rev%20(July%201).pdf (Accessed February 28, 2023).

Uvnas-Moberg, K. (2013). Short-term and long-term effects of oxytocin released by suckling and skin-to-skin contact in mothers and infants. In D. Narvaez, J. Panksepp, A. Schore, & T. Gleason, eds., *Evolution, Early Experience and Human Development: From Research to Practice and Policy.* Oxford University Press, pp. 299–306.

van IJzendoorn, M. H., Sagi, A., & Lambermon, M. W. E. (1992). The multiple caretaker paradox: Data from Holland and Israel. *New Directions for Child and Adolescent Development*, **57**, 5–24. https://doi.org/10.1002/cd.23219925703.

Van IJzendoorn, M. H., & Sagi, A. (1999). Cross-cultural patterns of attachment: Universal and contextual dimensions. In J. Cassidy & P. R. Shaver, eds., *Handbook of Attachment: Theory, Research, and Clinical Applications.* Guilford, pp. 713–734.

van Vliet, M. S., Mesman, J., Schultink, J. M. et al. (2022). Maternal sensitivity during mealtime and free play: Differences and explanatory factors. *Infancy*, **27(3)**, 630–644. https://doi.org/10.1111/infa.12465.

Victora, C., Vaughan, J. P., Lombardi, C. et al. (1987). Evidence for protection by breast-feeding against infant deaths from infectious diseases in Brazil. *The Lancet*, **330(8554)**, 319–322. https://doi.org/10.1016/S0140-6736(87)90902-0.

Veile, A. (2018). Hunter-gatherer diets and human behavioral evolution. *Physiology & Behavior*, **193**, 190–195. https://doi.org/10.1016/j.physbeh.2018.05.023.

Veile, A., & Miller, V. (2021). Duration of breast feeding in ancestral environments. In T. K. Shackelford & V. A. Weekes-Shackelford, eds., *Encyclopedia of Evolutionary Psychological Science.* Springer, pp. 2152–2156. https://doi.org/10.1007/978-3-319-19650-3_818.

Volk, A. A., & Atkinson, J. A. (2013). Infant and child death in the human environment of evolutionary adaptation. *Evolution and Human Behavior*, **34**, 182–192. https://doi.org/10.1016/j.evolhumbehav.2012.11.007.

Volk, T., & Atkinson, J. (2008). Is child death the crucible of human evolution? *Journal of Social, Evolutionary, and Cultural Psychology*, **2(4)**, 247. https://doi.org/10.1037/h0099341.

Volling, B. L., Gonzalez, R., Oh, W. et al. (2017). Developmental trajectories of children's adjustment across the transition to siblinghood: Pre-birth predictors and sibling outcomes at one year. *Monographs of the Society for Research in Child Development*, **82(3)**, 1–215. www.jstor.org/stable/45106959.

Volling, B. L., Oh, W., Gonzalez, R. et al. (2023). Changes in children's attachment security to mother and father after the birth of a sibling: Risk and resilience in the family. *Development and Psychopathology,* **35(3)**, 1404–1420. https://doi.org/10.1017/S0954579421001310.

Wambach, K., & Spencer, B. (2021). *Breastfeeding and Human Lactation,* 6th ed. Jones, Bartlett Learning Books.

Wang, E. T., Kodama, G., Baldi, P., & Moyzis, R. K. (2006). Global landscape of recent inferred Darwinian selection for Homo sapiens. *Proceedings of the National Academy of Sciences,* **103(1)**, 135–140. https://doi.org/10.1073/pnas.0509691102.

Warr, P. (2014). Food insecurity and its determinants. *Australian Journal of Agricultural and Resource Economics,* **58(4)**, 519–537. https://doi.org/10.1111/1467-8489.12073.

Waters, E., Kondo-Ikemura, K., Posada, G., & Richters, J. (1991). Learning to love: Mechanisms and milestones. In M. Gunner & Alan Sroufe, eds., *Minnesota Symposium on Child Psychology, Vol. 23: Self Processes and Development.* Erlbaum, pp. 217–255.

Waters-Rist, A. L., Bazaliiskii, V. I., Weber, A. W., & Katzenberg, M. A. (2011). Infant and child diet in Neolithic hunter-fisher-gatherers from Cis-Baikal, Siberia: Intra-long bone stable nitrogen and carbon isotope ratios. *American Journal of Physical Anthropology,* **146(2)**, 225–241. https://doi.org/10.1002/ajpa.21568.

White, A. A. (2014). Mortality, fertility, and the OY ratio in a model hunter–gatherer system. *American Journal of Physical Anthropology,* **154(2)**, 222–231. https://doi.org/10.1002/ajpa.22495.

Thousaddays.org (2023). Why 1,000 Days.thousanddays.org/why-1000-days/ (Accessed February 28, 2023).

Wilder, L., & Semendeferi, K. (2022). Infant brain development and plasticity from an evolutionary perspective. In S. L. Hart & D. F. Bjorklund, eds., *Evolutionary Perspectives on Infancy.* Springer, pp. 39–57. https://doi.org/10.1007/978-3-030-76000-7_3.

Williams, C. D. (1933). A nutritional disease of childhood associated with a maize diet. *Archives of Disease in Childhood,* **8(48)**, 423. https://doi.org/10.1136%2Fadc.8.48.423.

Williams, C. D., Oxon, B., & Lond, H. (1935). Kwashiorkor. A nutritional disease of children associated with a maize diet. *Lancet,* **5855**, 1151–1152. https://doi.org/10.1111/j.1753-4887.1973.tb07044.x.

Winnicott, D. W. (1977). *The Piggle: An Account of the Psychoanalytic Treatment of a Little Girl.* International Universities.

Winnicott, D. W. (2002). *Winnicott on the Child.* Perseus.

Włodarczyk, A., Elsner, C., Schmitterer, A., & Wertz, A. E. (2018). Every rose has its thorn: Infants' responses to pointed shapes in naturalistic contexts. *Evolution and Human Behavior*, **39(6),** 583–593. https://doi.org/10.1016/j.evolhumbehav.2018.06.001.

Wolraich, M. L., Felice, M. E. & Drotar, D. (1996). *The Classification of Child and Adolescent Mental Diagnoses in Primary Care: Diagnostic and Statistical Manual for Primary Care (DSM-PC) Child and Adolescent Version*. American Academy of Pediatrics.

World Health Organization (2023a). Stunting, wasting, overweight, and under weight.apps.who.int/nutrition/landscape/help.aspx?menu=0&helpid=391 &lang=EN (Accessed June 9, 2023).

World Health Organization (2023b). Infant and young child feeding. www.who.int/news-room/fact-sheets/detail/infant-and-young-child-feeding (Accessed February 2, 2023).

Worobey, J., Lopez, M. I., & Hoffman, D. J. (2009). Maternal behavior and infant weight gain in the first year. *Journal of Nutrition Education and Behavior*, **41(3)**, 169–175. https://doi.org/10.1016/j.jneb.2008.06.005.

Worthman, C. M. (2014). Survival and health. In M. H. Bornstein, ed., *Handbook of Cultural Developmental Science*. Psychology Press, pp. 39–59.

Yaya, S., Uthman, O. A., Ekholuenetale, M., Bishwajit, G., & Adjiwanou, V. (2020). Effects of birth spacing on adverse childhood health outcomes: Evidence from 34 countries in sub-Saharan Africa. *The Journal of Maternal-Fetal & Neonatal Medicine*, **33(20)**, 3501–3508. https://doi.org/10.1080/14767058.2019.1576623.

Zero-to-Three (2022). Why 0-3? wwwzerotothree.org/why-0-3/ (Accessed: November 16, 2022).

Zhu, D., Galbraith, E. D., Reyes-García, V., & Ciais, P. (2021). Global hunter-gatherer population densities constrained by influence of seasonality on diet composition. *Nature Ecology & Evolution*, **5(11)**, 1536–1545. https://doi.org/10.1038/s41559-021-01548-3.

Zucoloto, F. S. (2011). Evolution of the human feeding behavior. *Psychology & Neuroscience*, **4**, 131–141. https://doi.org/10.3922/j.psns.2011.1.015.

Cambridge Elements ≡

Applied Evolutionary Science

David F. Bjorklund
Florida Atlantic University

David F. Bjorklund is a Professor of Psychology at Florida Atlantic University in Boca Raton, Florida. He is the Editor-in-Chief of the *Journal of Experimental Child Psychology*, the Vice President of the Evolution Institute, and has written numerous articles and books on evolutionary developmental psychology, with a particular interest in the role of immaturity in evolution and development.

Editorial Board
David Buss, *University of Texas, Austin*
David Geary, *University of Missouri*
Mhairi Gibson, *University of Bristol*
Patricia Hawley, *Texas Tech University*
David Lancy, *Utah State University*
Jerome Lieberman, *Evolution Institute*
Todd Shackelford, *Oakland University*
Viviana Weeks-Shackelford, *Oakland University*
David Sloan Wilson, *SUNY Binghamton*
Nina Witoszek, *University of Oslo*
Rafael Wittek, *University of Groningen*

About the Series
This series presents original, concise, and authoritative reviews of key topics in applied evolutionary science. Highlighting how an evolutionary approach can be applied to real-world social issues, many Elements in this series will include findings from programs that have produced positive educational, social, economic, or behavioral benefits. Cambridge Elements in Applied Evolutionary Science is published in association with the Evolution Institute.

 THE EVOLUTION INSTITUTE

Cambridge Elements $\equiv$

Applied Evolutionary Science

Elements in the Series

A full series listing is available at: www.cambridge.org/EAES.

.

Printed in the United States
by Baker & Taylor Publisher Services